Anonymous

Regulations for the Army of the Confederate States,

And for the Quartermaster's Department and Pay Department

Anonymous

Regulations for the Army of the Confederate States,
And for the Quartermaster's Department and Pay Department

ISBN/EAN: 9783337713652

Printed in Europe, USA, Canada, Australia, Japan

Cover: Foto ©ninafisch / pixelio.de

More available books at **www.hansebooks.com**

REGULATIONS

FOR THE

ARMY OF THE CONFEDERATE STATES,

AND FOR THE

QUARTERMASTER'S DEPARTMENT

AND

PAY DEPARTMENT.

WAR DEPARTMENT,
MONTGOMERY, APRIL, 1861.

The following Regulations for the Quartermaster's Department and Pay Department, and the accompanying General Regulations in regard to public property, money and accounts, the duties of commanding officers, and working parties, having been approved by the PRESIDENT, he commands that they be published for the government of all concerned, and that they be strictly observed. Nothing contrary to the tenor of these present Regulations will be enjoined or allowed, in any part of the forces of the Confederate States, by any commander whatsoever.

L. P. WALKER,
Secretary of War

REGULATIONS

FOR THE

ARMY OF THE CONFEDERATE STATES.

QUARTERMASTER GENERAL'S OFFICE,
MONTGOMERY, ALA., May 11, 1861.

Until further orders the following will be the only monthly reports required at this office, viz:

Estimates—with list of outstanding debts, if any.

Monthly Summary Statement.

Report of Persons and Articles hired, &c.

Muster Rolls of Extra Duty Men.

Report of Stores transported.

List of Quarters and Fuel commuted, (Form 7.)

NOTE.—All papers for Quartermaster General to be sent by letter, and in every instance care will be taken to give the postoffice, county and State. This is necessary to insure prompt reply.

QUARTERMASTER'S DEPARTMENT.

1. This department provides the quarters and transportation of the army; storage and transportation for all army supplies; army clothing; camp and garrison equipage; cavalry and artillery horses; fuel; forage; straw, and stationery.

2. The incidental expenses of the army paid through the Quartermaster's Department include per diem to extra-duty men; postage on public service; the expenses of courts-martial, of the pursuit and apprehension of deserters, of the burials of officers and soldiers, of hired escorts, of expresses, interpreters, spies, and guides, of veterinary surgeons and medicine for horses, and of supplying posts with water; and generally the proper and authorized expenses for the movements and operations of an army not expressly assigned to any other department.

BARRACKS AND QUARTERS.

3. Under this head are included the permanent buildings for the use of the army, as barracks, quarters, hospital, storehouses, offices, stables.

4. When barracks and quarters are to be occupied, they will be allotted by the Quartermaster at the station, under the control of the commanding officer.

5. The number of rooms and amount of fuel for officers and men are as follows :

	Rooms.			Cords of wood per month.*	
	As quarters.	As kitchen.	As office.	From May 1, to Sept. 30.	From Oct. 1, to April 30.
A Brigadier-General or Colonel, ...	4	1	..	1	4
A Lieutenant-Colonel or Major, ...	3	1	..	1	3½
A Captain or Chaplain, ...	2	1	..	¾	3
Lieutenant	1	1	.	½	2
The General commanding the army	..	.	3	..	3
The commanding officer of a division or department, an assistant or deputy Quartermaster General....	.	..	2	..	2
The commanding officer of a regiment or post, Quartermaster, Assistant Quartermaster, or Commissary of Subsistence...	..	..	1	..	1
An acting Assistant Quartermaster when approved by the Quartermaster General.....	..	..	.	..	..
Wagon and forage master, Sergeant-Major, Ordnance Sergeant, or Quartermaster Sergeant,...........	1	.	..	½	1
Each non-commissioned officer, musician, private, [redacted] and washerwoman	..	.	.	1–12	1–6
Each necessary fire for the sick in hospital, to be regulated by the surgeon and commanding officer, *not exceeding*....	..	..	..	½	2
Each guard-fire, to be regulated by the commanding officer, *not exceeding*	.	..	..	..	3
A commissary or quartermaster's storehouse when necessary, *not exceeding*	..	..	..	.	1
A regiment or post mess...........	1	..	..	.	1
To every six non-commissioned officers, musicians, privates, and washerwomen, 256 square feet of room.....					

* Or coal, at the rate of 1,500 pounds anthracite, or 30 bushels bituminous to the cord.

TABLE OF DAILY ALLOWANCE OF FUEL.

Days.	1-12 cord per month.		Days.	1-6 cord per month.		Days.	½ cord per month.		Days.	¾ cord per month.		Days.	1 cord per month.			Days.	2 cords per month.			Days.	3 cords per month.			Days.	3½ cords per month.			Days.	4 cords per month.		
	Cubic feet.	Inches.		Cubic feet.	Inches.		Cubic feet.	Inches.		Cubic feet.	Inch.		Cords	Cubic feet.	Inches.		Cords	Cubic feet.	Inches.		Cords	Cubic feet.	Inches.		Cords	Cubic feet.	Inches.		Cords	Cubic feet.	Inches.
1		4	1		8	1	2	1	1	3	2	1		4	3	1		8	6	1		12	9	1		14	11	1		17	
2		8	2	1	5	2	4	3	2	6	4	2		8	6	2		17	0	2		25	7	2		29	10	2		34	1
3	1	0	3	2	1	3	6	4	3	9	7	3		12	9	3		25	7	3		38	4	3		44	9	3		51	2
4	1	5	4	2	10	4	8	6	4	12	9	4		17	0	4		34	1	4		51	2	4		59	8	4		68	3
5	1	9	5	3	6	5	10	8	5	16	0	5		21	4	5		42	8	5		64	0	5		74	8	5		85	4
6	2	1	6	4	3	6	12	9	6	19	2	6		25	7	6		51	2	6		76	9	6		89	7	6		102	4
7	2	5	7	4	11	7	14	11	7	22	4	7		29	10	7		59	8	7		89	7	7		104	6	7		119	5
8	2	10	8	5	7	8	17	0	8	25	7	8		34	1	8		68	3	8		102	4	8		119	5	8	1	8	6
9	3	2	9	6	3	9	19	2	9	28	9	9		38	4	9		76	9	9		115	2	9	1	6	4	9	1	25	7
10	3	6	10	7	0	10	21	4	10	32	0	10		42	8	10		85	4	10	1			10	1	21	4	10	1	42	8
11	3	10	11	7	8	11	23	5	11	35	2	11		46	11	11		93	10	11	1	12	9	11	1	36	3	11	1	59	8
12	4	3	12	8	5	12	25	7	12	38	4	12		51	2	12		102	4	12	1	25	7	12	1	51	2	12	1	76	9
13	4	7	13	9	2	13	27	8	13	41	7	13		55	5	13		110	11	13	1	38	4	13	1	66	1	13	1	93	10
14	4	11	14	9	11	14	29	10	14	44	9	14		59	8	14		119	5	14	1	51	2	14	1	81	0	14	1	110	11
15	5	4	15	10	8	15	32	0	15	48	0	15		64	0	15	1	0	0	15	1	64	0	15	1	96	0	15	2	0	0
16	5	8	16	11	4	16	34	1	16	51	2	16		68	3	16	1	8	6	16	1	76	9	16	1	110	11	16	2	17	0
17	6	0	17	12	1	17	36	3	17	54	4	17		72	6	17	1	17	0	17	1	89	7	17	1	125	10	17	2	34	1
18	6	4	18	12	9	18	38	4	18	57	7	18		76	9	18	1	25	7	18	1	102	4	18	2	12	9	18	2	51	2
19	6	9	19	13	6	19	40	6	19	60	9	19		81	0	19	1	34	1	19	1	115	2	19	2	27	8	19	2	68	3
20	7	1	20	14	2	20	42	8	20	64	0	20		85	4	20	1	42	8	20	2			20	2	42	8	20	2	85	4
21	7	5	21	14	11	21	44	9	21	67	2	21		89	7	21	1	51	2	21	2	12	9	21	2	57	7	21	2	102	4
22	7	9	22	15	7	22	46	11	22	70	4	22		93	10	22	1	59	8	22	2	25	7	22	2	72	6	22	2	119	5
23	8	2	23	16	4	23	49	0	23	73	7	23		98	1	23	1	68	3	23	2	38	4	23	2	87	5	23	3	8	6
24	8	6	24	17	0	24	51	2	24	76	9	24		102	4	24	1	76	9	24	2	51	2	24	2	102	4	24	3	25	7
25	8	10	25	17	9	25	53	3	25	80	0	25		106	8	25	1	85	4	25	2	64	0	25	2	117	4	25	3	42	8
26	9	2	26	18	5	26	55	5	26	83	2	26		110	11	26	1	93	10	26	2	76	9	26	3	4	3	26	3	59	8
27	9	7	27	19	2	27	57	7	27	86	4	27		115	2	27	1	102	4	27	2	89	7	27	3	19	2	27	3	76	9
28	9	11	28	19	10	28	59	8	28	89	7	28		119	5	28	1	110	11	28	2	102	4	28	3	34	1	28	3	93	10
29	10	3	29	20	7	29	61	10	29	92	9	29		123	8	29	1	119	5	29	2	115	2	29	3	49	0	29	3	110	11
30	10	8	30	21	4	30	64	0	30	96	0	30	1			30	2			30	3			30	3	64	0	30	4		

6. Merchantable hard wood is the standard; the cord is 128 cubic feet.

7. No officer shall occupy more than his proper quarters, except by order of the commanding officer when there is an excess of quarters at the station; which order the quartermaster shall forward to the Quartermaster General, to be laid before the Secretary of War. But the amount of quarters shall be reduced pro rata by the commanding officer when the number of officers and troops make it necessary; and when the public buildings are not sufficient to quarter the troops, the commanding officer shall report to the commander of the department for authority to hire quarters, or other necessary orders therein, to the Quartermaster General.

8. A mess-room, and fuel for it, are allowed only when a majority of the officers of a post or regiment unite in a mess; never to less than three officers, nor to any who live in hotels or boarding-houses. Fuel for a mess-room shall not be used elsewhere, or for any other purpose.

9. Fuel issued to officers or troops is public property for their use; what they do not actually consume shall be returned to the quartermaster and taken up on his quarterly return.

10. Fuel shall be issued only in the month when due.

11. In allotting quarters, officers shall have choice according to rank, but the commanding officer may direct the officers to be stationed convenient to their troops.

12. An officer may select quarters occupied by a junior; but, having made his choice, he must abide by it, and shall not again at the post displace a junior, unless himself displaced by a senior.

13. The set of rooms to each quarters will be assigned by the quartermaster, under the control of the commanding officer; attics not counted as rooms.

14. Officers cannot choose rooms in different sets of quarters.

15. When public quarters cannot be furnished to officers at stations without troops, or to enlisted men at general or department head-quarters, quarters will be commuted at a rate fixed by the Secretary of War, and fuel at the market price delivered. When fuel and quarters are commuted to an officer by reason of his employment on a civil work, the commutation shall be charged to the appropriation for the work. No commutation of rooms or fuel is allowed for offices or messes.

16. An officer is not deprived of his quarters and fuel, or commutation, at his station, by temporary absence on duty.

17. Officers and troops in the field are not entitled to commutation for quarters or fuel.

18. An officer arriving at a station shall make requisition on the quartermaster for his quarters and fuel, accompanied by a copy of the order putting him on duty at the station. If in command of troops, his requisition shall be for the whole, and designate the number of officers of each grade, of non-commissioned officers, soldiers, and washerwomen.

19. Bunks, benches, and tables provided for soldiers' barracks and hospitals, are not to be removed from them, except by the quartermaster of the station, or order of the commanding officers, and shall not be removed from the station except by order of the Quartermaster General.

20. The furniture for each office will be two common desks or tables, six common chairs, one pair common andirons, and shovel and tongs.

21. Furniture will be provided for officers' quarters when special appropriations for that purpose are made. Sales to officers of materials for furniture may be made at cost, at posts where they cannot be otherwise obtained.

22. When buildings are to be occupied or allotted, an inspection of them shall be made by the commanding officer and quartermaster. Statements, in triplicate, of their condition, and of the fixtures and furniture in each room, shall be made by the quartermaster, and revised by the commanding officer. One of these shall be retained by the commanding officer, one by the quartermaster, and the third forwarded to the Quartermaster General.

23. Like inspection of all buildings in the use of troops will be made at the monthly inspections of the troops, and of all buildings which have been in the use of officers or troops, whenever vacated by them. Damages will be promptly repaired if the quartermaster has the means. Commanding officers will take notice, as a military offence, of any neglect by any officer or soldier to take proper care of the rooms or furniture in his use or occupancy; but such officer or soldier may be allowed to pay the cost of the repairs when the commanding officer deems that sufficient in the case. Commanding officers are required to report to the Quartermaster General their proceedings in all cases of neglect under this regulation.

24. An annual inspection of the public buildings at the several stations shall be made at the end of June by the commanding officer and quartermaster, and then the quartermaster

shall make the following reports: 1st. of the condition and capacity of the buildings, and of the additions, alterations and repairs that have been made during the past year; 2d. of the additions, alterations and repairs that are needed, with plans and estimates in detail.

These reports the commanding officer shall examine and forward, with his views, to the Quartermaster General.

25. Necessary repairs of public buildings, not provided for in the appropriations, can only be made by the labor of the troops.

26. When private buildings occupied as barracks or quarters, or lands occupied for encampments, are vacated, the commanding officer and quartermaster shall make an inspection of them, and a report to the Quartermaster General of their condition, and of any injury to them by the use of the Confederate States.

27. Military posts evacuated by the troops, and lands reserved for military use, will be put in charge of the Quartermaster's Department, unless otherwise specially ordered.

ARMY TRANSPORTATION.

28. When troops are moved, or officers travel with escorts or stores, the means of transport provided shall be for the whole command. Proper orders in the case, and an exact return of the command, including company women, will be furnished to the quartermaster who is to provide the transportation.

29. The baggage to be transported is limited to camp and garrison equipage, and officers' baggage. Officers' baggage shall not exceed (mess-chest and all personal effects included) as follows:

	In the field.	Changing stations.
General officers, - - -	125 pounds.	1000 pounds.
Field officers, - - - -	100 "	800 "
Captains, - - - -	80 "	700 "
Subalterns, - - - -	80 "	600 "

These amounts shall be reduced *pro rata* by the commanding officer when necessary, and may be increased by the Quartermaster General on transports by water, when proper, in special cases.

30. The regimental and company desk prescribed in army regulations will be transported; also for staff officers, the books,

papers, and instruments necessary to their duties; and for medical officers, their medical chest. In doubtful cases under this regulation, and whenever baggage exceeds the regulated allowance, the conductor of the train, or officer in charge of the transportation, will report to the commanding officer, who will order an inspection, and all excesses to be rejected.

31. Estimates of the medical director, approved by the commanding officer, for the necessary transportation to be provided for the hospital service, will be furnished to the quartermaster.

32. The sick will be transported on the application of the medical officers.

33. Certified invoices of all public stores to be transported will be furnished to the quartermaster by the officer having charge of them. In doubtful cases, the orders of the commanding officer will be required.

34. Where officers' horses are to be transported, it must be authorized in the orders for the movement.

35. The baggage trains, ambulances, and all the means of transport continue in charge of the proper officers of the Quartermaster's Department, under the control of the commanding officers.

36. In all cases of transportation, whether of troops or stores, an exact return of the amount and kind of transportation employed will be made by the quartermaster to the Quartermaster General, accompanied by the orders for the movement, a return of the troops, and an invoice of the stores.

37. Wagons and their equipments for the transport service of the army will be procured, when practicable, from the Ordnance Department, and fabricated in the government establishments.

38. When army supplies are turned over to a quartermaster for transportation, each package shall be directed and its contents marked on it; and duplicate invoices and receipts in bulk will be exchanged between the issuing and forwarding officer.

39. On transports, cabin passage will be provided for officers, and reasonable and proper accommodation for the troops, and, when possible, a separate apartment for the sick.

40. An officer who travels not less than ten miles without troops, escort, or military stores, and under special orders in the case from a superior, or a summons to attend a military court, shall receive ten cents mileage, or, if he prefer it, the actual cost of his transportation and of the transportation of his allowance of baggage for the whole journey, provided he has

traveled in the customary reasonable manner. Mileage will not be allowed where the travel is by government conveyances, which will be furnished in case of necessity.

41. If the journey be to cash treasury drafts, the necessary and actual cost of transportation only will be allowed; and the account must describe the draft and state its amount, and set out the items of expense, and be supported by a certificate that the journey was necessary to procure specie for the draft at par.

42. If an officer shall travel on urgent public duty without orders, he shall report the case to the superior who had authority to order the journey; and his approval, if then given, shall allow the actual cost of transportation. Mileage is computed by the shortest mail route, and the distance by the General Post-Office book. When the distance cannot be so ascertained, it shall be reckoned subject to the decision of the Quartermaster General.

43. Orders to an officer on leave of absence to rejoin the station or troops he left, will not carry transportation.

44. Citizens receiving military appointments join their stations without expense to the public.

45. But assistant surgeons approved by an examining board and commissioned, receive transportation in the execution of their first order to duty, and graduates of the Military Academy receive transportation from the academy to their stations.

46. When officers are permitted to exchange stations, the public will not be put to expense of transportation, which would have been saved if such exchange had not been permitted.

47. A paymaster's clerk will receive the actual expenses of his transportation while travelling under orders in the discharge of his duty, upon his affidavit to the account of expenses, and the certificate of the paymaster that the journey was on duty.

48. Travel of officers on business of civil works will be charged to the appropriation for the work.

49. No officer shall have orders to attend personally at the seat of government, to the settlement of his accounts, except by order of the Secretary of War on the report of the bureau, or of the Treasury, showing a necessity therefor.

FORAGE.

50. The forage ration is fourteen pounds of hay and twelve pounds of oats, corn or barley.

51. In time of war officers of the army shall be entitled to

draw forage for horses according to grade, as follows: A Brigadier General four; the Adjutant and Inspector General, Quartermaster General, Commissary General, and the Colonels of Engineers, Artillery and Cavalry, three each. All Lieutenant-Colonels, and Majors, and Captains of the general staff, Engineer Corps, Light Artillery and Cavalry, three each. Lieutenants serving in the Corps of Engineers, Lieutenants of Light Artillery and of Cavalry, two each. In time of peace, general and field officers, three. Officers below the rank of field officers in the general staff, Corps of Engineers, Light Artillery and Cavalry, two. Aids-de-camp and Adjutant's forage for the same number of horses as allowed to officers of the same grade in the mounted service, in time of war and peace: provided in all cases, that the horses are actually kept in service and mustered. No enlisted man in the service of the Confederate States, shall be employed as a servant by any officer of the army.

52. No officer shall sell forage issued to him. Forage issued to public horses or cattle is public property; what they do not actually consume to be properly accounted for.

STRAW.

53. In barracks, twelve pounds of straw per month for bedding will be allowed to each man, and company woman.

54. The allowance and change of straw for the sick is regulated by the surgeon.

55. One hundred pounds per month is allowed for bedding to each horse in public service.

56. At posts near prairie land owned by the Confederate States, hay will be used instead of straw, and provided by the troops.

Straw not actually used as bedding shall be accounted for as other public property.

STATIONERY.

57. Issues of stationery are made quarterly, in amount as follows:

	Quires of writing paper.	Quires of envelope paper.	Number of quills.	Ounces of wafers.	Ounces of sealing wax.	Papers of ink powders.	Pieces of office tape.
Commander of an army, department, or division, (what may be necessary for himself and staff for their public duty.)							
Commander of a brigade, for himself and staff,	12	1	50	1	8	2	2
Officer commanding a regiment or post of not less than five companies for himself and staff,	10	1	40	1	6	2	1
Officer commanding a post of more than two and less than five companies,	8	½	30	½	5	1	1
Commanding officer of a post of two companies,	6	½	25	½	4	1	1
Commanding officer of a post of one company or less, and commanding officer of a company,	5	½	20	½	3	1	1
A Lieutenant Colonel or Major not in command of a regiment or post,	3	¼	12	¼	2	1	1
Officers of the Inspector-General's, Pay and Quartermaster's Department (the prescribed blank books and printed forms, and the stationery required for their public duty).							
All officers, including Chaplains, not enumerated above, when on duty and not supplied by their respective departments,	1½	⅓	6	¼	1	½	½

Steel pens, with one holder, to 12 pens, may be issued in place of quills, and envelopes in place of envelope paper, at the rate of 100 to the quire.

58. When an officer is relieved in command, he shall transfer the office stationery to his successor.

59. To each office table is allowed one inkstand, one stamp, one paper folder, one sand-box, one wafer-box, and as many lead pencils as may be required, not exceeding four per annum.

60. Necessary stationery for military courts and boards will be furnished on the requisition of the recorder, approved by the presiding officer.

61. The commander of an army, department or division, may direct orders to be printed, when the requisite dispatch and the number to be distributed make it necessary. The necessity will be set out in the order for the printing, or certified on the account.

62. Regimental, company, and post books, and printed blanks for the officers of Quartermaster and Pay Departments, will be procured by timely requisition on the Quartermaster General.

63. Printed matter procured by the Quartermaster General for use out of . may be procured elsewhere, at a cost not to exceed the rates prescribed by Congress for the public printing, increased by the cost of transportation.

EXPENSES OF COURTS-MARTIAL.

64. An officer who attends a general court-martial or court of inquiry, convened by authority competent to order a general court-martial, will be paid, if the court is not held at the station where he is at the time serving, one dollar a day while attending the court and travelling to and from it if entitled to forage, and one dollar and twenty-five cents a day if not entitled to forage.

65. The Judge Advocate or Recorder will be paid, besides, a per diem of one dollar and twenty-five cents for every day he is necessarily employed in the duty of the court. When it is necessary to employ a clerk to aid the Judge Advocate, the court may order it; a soldier to be procured when practicable.

66. A citizen witness shall be paid his actual transportation or stage fare, and three dollars a day while attending the court and travelling to and from it, counting the travel at fifty miles a day.

67. The certificate of the Judge Advocate shall be evidence of the time of attendance on the court, and of the time he was necessarily employed in the duty of the court. Of the time occupied in travelling, each officer will make his own certificate.

EXTRA-DUTY MEN.

68. Duplicate rolls of the extra-duty men, to be paid by the Quartermaster's Department, will be made monthly, and certified by the quartermaster, or other officer having charge of the work, and countersigned by the commanding officer. One of these will be transmitted direct to the Quartermaster General, and the other filed in support of the pay-roll.

PUBLIC POSTAGE.

69. Postage and despatches by telegraph, on public business, paid by an officer, will be refunded to him on his certificate to the account, and to the necessity of the communication by telegraph. The amount for postage, and for telegraph despatches, will be stated separately.

HORSES FOR MOUNTED OFFICERS.

70. In the field, or on the frontier, the commanding officer may authorize a mounted officer, who cannot otherwise provide himself with two horses, to take them from the public at the cost price, when it can be ascertained, and when not, at a fair valuation, to be fixed by a board of survey, provided he shall not take the horse of any trooper. A horse so taken shall not be exchanged or returned. Horses of mounted officers shall be shod by the public farrier or blacksmith.

CLOTHING, CAMP AND GARRISON EQUIPAGE.

71. Supplies of clothing and camp and garrison equipage will be sent by the Quartermaster General from the general depot to the officers of his department stationed with the troops.

72. The contents of each package, and the size of clothing in it, will be marked on it.

73. The receiving quartermaster will give duplicate receipts for the clothing as invoiced to him, if the packages as received and marked agree with the invoice, and appear rightly marked, and in good order; if otherwise, an inspection will be made by a board of survey, whose report in case of damage or deficiency will be transmitted, one copy to the Quartermaster General and one to the officer forwarding the supplies. In case of damage, the board will assess the damage to each article.

74. ALLOWANCE OF CAMP AND GARRISON EQUIPAGE.

	Tents in the field.	Spades.	Axes.	Pickaxes.	Hatchets.	Camp kettles.	Mess pans.
A General,	3		1		1		
Field or staff officer above the rank of Captain,	2		1		1		
Other staff officers or Captains,	1		1		1		
Subalterns of a company, to every two,	1		1		1		
To every 15 foot and 13 mounted men,	1	2	2	2	2	2	5

75. Bed-sacks are provided for troops in garrison, and iron pots may be furnished to them instead of camp kettles. On the march and in the field, the only mess furniture of the soldier will be one tin plate, one tin cup, one knife, fork and spoon, to each man, to be carried by himself on the march. Requisitions will be sent to the Quartermaster General for the authorized flags, colors, standards, guidons, drums, fifes, bugles and trumpets.

ALLOWANCE FOR CLOTHING.

76. A soldier is allowed the uniform clothing stated in the following table, or articles thereof of equal value. When a balance is due him at the end of a year, it is added to his allowance for the next.

CLOTHING.	FOR THREE YEARS. 1st.	2d.	3d.	Total in the three years.
Cap, complete,	2	1	1	4
Cover,	1	1	1	3
Coat,	2	1	1	4
Trowsers,	3	2	2	7
Flannel shirts,	3	3	3	9
" drawers,	3	2	2	7
Bootees,* pairs,	4	4	4	12
Stockings, pairs,	4	4	4	12
Leather stock,	1			1
Great coat,	1			1
Stable frock (for mounted men,)	1			1
Fatigue overall (for engineers and ordnance,)	1	1	1	3
Blanket,	1		1	2

77. One sash is allowed to each company for the first sergeant. This and the metalic scales, letters, numbers, castles, shells, and flames, and the camp and garrison equipage, will not be returned as issued, but borne on the return while fit for service. They will be charged to the person in whose use they are, when lost or destroyed by his fault.

78. Commanders of companies draw the clothing of their men, and the camp and garrison equipage for the officers and

* Mounted men may receive *one* pair of "boots" and *two* pair of "bootees," instead of *four* pairs of bootees.

men of their company. The camp and garrison equipage of other officers is drawn on their own receipts.

79. When clothing is needed for issue to the men, the company commander will procure it from the quartermaster on requisition, approved by the commanding officer.

80. Ordinarily the company commander will procure and issue clothing to his men twice a year; at other times, when necessary in special cases.

81. Such articles of clothing as the soldier may need will be issued to him. When the issues equal in value his allowance for the year, further issues are extra issues, to be charged to him on the next muster-roll.

82. The money value of the clothing, and of each article of it, will be ascertained annually, and announced in orders from the War Department.

83. Officers receiving clothing, or camp and garrison equipage, will render quarterly returns to the Quartermaster General.

84. Commanders of companies will take the receipts of their men for the clothing issued to them, on a receipt roll, witnessed by an officer, or in the absence of an officer, by a non-commissioned officer; the witness to be witness to the fact of the issue and the acknowledgment and signature of the soldier. The several issues to a soldier to be entered separately on the roll, and all vacant spaces on the roll to be filled with a cipher. This roll is the voucher for the issue to the quarterly return of the company commander. Extra issues will be so noted on the roll.

85. Each soldier's clothing account is kept by the company commander in a company book. This account sets out only the money value of the clothing which he received at each issue, for which his receipt is entered in the book, and witnessed as in the preceding paragraph.

86. When a soldier is transferred or detached, the amount due to or by him on account of clothing will be stated on his descriptive list.

87. When a soldier is discharged, the amount due to or by him for clothing will be stated on the duplicate certificates given for the settlement of his accounts.

88. Deserters' clothing will be turned into store. The invoice of it, and the quartermaster's receipt for it, will state its condition and the name of the deserter.

89. The inspection report on damaged clothing shall set out,

with the amount of damage to each article, a list of such articles as are fit for issue, at a reduced price stated.

90. Commanding officers may order necessary issues of clothing to prisoners and convicts, taking deserters' or other damaged clothing when there is such in store.

91. In all cases of deficiency, or damage of any article of clothing, or camp or garrison equipage, the officer accountable for the property is required by law "to show by one or more depositions setting forth the circumstances of the case, that the deficiency was by unavoidable accident or loss in actual service, without any fault on his part, and in case of damage, that due care and attention were exerted on his part, and that the damage did not result from neglect."

RETURNS IN THE QUARTERMASTER'S DEPARTMENT.

92. All officers and agents having money and property of the Department to account for, are required to make the monthly and quarterly returns to the Quartermaster General prescribed in the following articles:

93. Monthly returns, to be transmitted within five days after the month to which they relate, viz: A summary statement (Form 1;) report of persons and things (Form 2;) roll of extra-duty men (Form 3); report of stores for transportation, &c. (Form 4); return of animals, wagons, harness, &c. (Form 5); report of forage (Form 6); report of fuel and quarters commuted (Form 7); report of pay due (Form 8); an estimate of funds for one month (Form 9) will be sent with the monthly returns. It will be for the current month, or such subsequent month as may give time to receive the remittance. Other special estimates will be transmitted when necessary.

94. Quarterly returns, to be transmitted within twenty days after the quarter to which they relate, viz: An account current of money (Form 10,) with abstracts and vouchers, as shown in Forms Nos. 11 to 22; a return of property (Form 23,) with abstract and vouchers, as shown in Forms Nos. 24 to 45; a duplicate of the property return without abstracts or vouchers; and a quarterly statement of the allowances paid to officers (Form 46.)

95. A distinct account current will be returned of money received and disbursed under the appropriation for "contingencies of the army." (See Forms Nos. 47, 48, and 22, for the forms of the account current, abstracts, and vouchers.) Necessary

expenditures by the quartermaster for the Medical Department are entered on abstract C. (See Forms 49 and 50.) The account will, ordinarily, be transferred from "army contingencies" to the appropriation for the Medical and Hospital Department, in the Treasury.

96. Forms 51 and 52 are the forms of the quarterly returns of clothing, camp and garrison equipage, and the receipt roll of issues to soldiers.

97. When persons and articles hired in the Quartermaster's Department are transferred, a descriptive list (Form 53) will be forwarded with them to the quartermaster to whom they are sent.

98. Officers serving in the Quartermaster's Department will report to the Quartermaster General useful information in regard to the routes and means of transportation and of supplies.

No. 1.

MONTHLY SUMMARY STATEMENT.

The Confederate States in account with ———, *at* ———, *in the month of* ——— 186 .

Dr.			Cr.		
To amount of purchases within the month,			By balance per last statement, . .		
To amount of expenditures within the month, ...			By cash received from ———, . .		
To amount of advances made to officers, per abstract, ...			By cash received from the Treasurer of the Confederate States, being amount of warrant No. —, ...		
Balance due the Confederate States, carried to next statement, ...					
$			$		

I certify that the above is a true statement of all the moneys which have come into my hands, on account of the Quartermaster's Department, during the month of ——— 186 , and that the disbursements have been faithfully made. The balance due the Confederate States is deposited in ———.

A. B., *Quartermaster.*

Note—No vouchers accompany this statement; abstracts of advances or transfers only, when the number of them makes the abstract necessary.

No. 2.

Report of Persons and Articles employed and hired at

Running Numbers.	No of each class.	Names of persons and articles.	Designation and occupation.	Service during the month. From.	To.	Day.	Rates of hire or compensation. Amount.	Day, month, or voyage.	Date of contract, agreement, or entry into service.
1	1	House, 3 rooms,	Quarters,	1	31	31	$40 00	Month,	July 1, 1850,
2	2	House, 4 rooms,	Store-ho'se,	3	31	31	31 00	Month,	Dec. 3, 1849,
3	3	House, 2 rooms,	Guard-ho'e,	1	31	31	19 00	Montl',	Dec. 3, 1840,
1	1	Ship Fanny,	Transport,	1	31	31	22000 00	Voyage,	May 3, 1850,
2	2	Schr. Heroine,	Transport,	1	31	31	700 00	Month,	June 4, 1850,
1	1	Wagon and team,	. . .	1	31	31	100 00	Month,	Jan. 1, 1850,
l	1	Chas. James,	Clerk,	1	31	31	75 00	Month,	Dec. 3, 1850,
2	1	Isaac Lowd,	Interpreter,	7	10	4	2 00	Day,	Jan. 7, 1851,
3	1	Peter Keene,	Express,	7	12	9	40 00	Month,	Jan. 7, 1851,
4	1	John Peters,	Blacksmith,	22	31	7	2 00	Day,	Jan. 1, 1851,
5	1	Thos. Cross,	Laborer,	1	31	31	20 00	Month,	May 3, 1850,
		Confederate States Steamer Fashion.							
1	1	Jas. Corwin,	Captain,	1	31	3	150 00	Month,	Dec. 1, 1850,
2	1	Geo. Pratt,	Engineer,	1	31	3	100 00	Month,	Dec. 1, 1850,
3	1	John Paul,	Mate,	1	31	3	50 00	Month,	Dec. 1, 1850,

Amount of rent and hire during the month, ...

I certify, on honor, that the above is a true report of all the persons and arti-
the observations under the head of Remarks, and the statement of amounts
Examined

C. D.,
Commanding.

No. 2.

——. *during the month of* —— 186 , *by* ——.

By whom owned.	Amount of rent or pay in the month.	Remarks showing by whom the buildings were occupied, and for what purpose, and how the vessels and men were employed during the month. (Transfers and discharges will be noted under this head.)	Time and amount due and remaining unpaid. From.	To.	Am't.
			1860.	1861.	
A. Byrne,	$40 00	Major 3d Infantry, . .	Dec. 1,	Jan. 31,	$ 80 00
Jas. Black,	29 00	Subsistence Store and Office.	Dec. 3.	Jan. 31,	60 00
Jas. Black,	10 00	Companies I & K, 3d Infantry.			
G. Wilkins,	. .	Transporting stores to Benicia,	Voy'ge	not com	pleted
			1861.	1861.	
T. Browne,	700 00	Transporting stores to Brazos,	Jan. 1,	Jan. 31,	700 00
Jas. Barry,	100 00	Hauling stores to San Antonio,	Jan. 1,	Jan. 31,	100 00
	75 00	Quartermaster's Office.			
	8 00	Employed by Com'ing General.			
	7 74	Express to Indianola.			
	14 00	Shoeing public horses.			
	20 00	Helping blacksmith.			
	150 00	Steamship sent to Brazos,	July 1,	July 31.	150 00
	100 00	Steamship sent to Brazos,	July 1,	July 31.	100 00
	50 00	Steamship sent to Brazos,	July 1.	July 31.	50 00
. .	1303 74	Total amount due and remaining unpaid.			1240 00

cles employed and hired by me during the month of ——, 186 , and that due and remaining unpaid are correct.

E. F.,

Asst. Qr. Master.

No. 3.

Roll of Non-commissioned Officers and Privates employed on extra duty, as Mechanics and Laborers, at ——, during the month of ——— 186 , by ——.

No.	Names.	Rank or designation.	Company.	Regiment.	By whose order employed.	Nature of service.	Term of service.			Rate of pay, or compensation.			How employed.
							From.	To.	No. days.	Per diem. Cents.	Dolls.	Cts.	REMARKS.
										$			

I certify that the above is a correct roll of non-commissioned officers, musicans and privates, employed on extra duty, under my direction, during the month of ——— 186 , and that the remarks opposite their names are accurate and just.

A. B.,
Quartermaster (or officer commanding)

Examined. C. D., *Commanding.*

No. 4.

Report of Stores received for Transportation and Distribution at ——, by ——, in the month of —— 186 .

Time received.	Marks.	No.	Contents.	From whom received.	By whom received.	Time sent.	To whom sent, and where	With whom sent.	Intermediate destination.	Ultimate destination.	Remarks.
186 June 1	W. S., &c.	1 to 3	Clothing.	Capt. A. B., Asst. Quartermaster.	Sloop Sally, Capt. A. W.	186	Capt. C., Asst. Quartermaster.	Ship George, Capt. I. B.	....	....	Received in good order.

I certify that the above report is correct

E. A. O., *Quartermaster*

No. 5.

Monthly Return of Public Animals, Wagons, Harness, and other means of Transportation in the possession of ——, *at* ——, *during the month of* —— 186 .

Date.		Horses.	Mules.	Oxen.	Wagons.	Ambulances.	Carts.	Wheel harness, single sets of.	Lead harness, single sets of.	Wagon saddles.	Ships.	Schooners.	Sloops.	Steamers.	Boats and barges.	Skiffs and batteaux.	Remarks.
	On hand, . . .																18 horses purchased; average cost $——.
	Purchased during the month, .																Wagons purchased at ——.
	Received from officers, . .																6 horses received from ——.
	Total to be accounted for, .																
	Transferred, . . .																Horses transferred to ——.
	Sold and worn out, . .																Wagons transferred to ——.
	Died and lost, . . .																1 horse sold;—horses died on the road to ——.
	Total issued and expended, .																
	Remaining on hand, .																

I certify that the above return is correct.

A. B., *Quartermaster.*

NOTE.—No other articles than those above enumerated will be placed on this return.

No. 6.

Monthly Report of Forage which has been issued to Horses, Mules, and Oxen in the public service at ——, by ——, during the month of —— 186 .

Date	To whom issued.	Public. Horses.	Public. Mules.	Public. Oxen.	Private. Horses.	Private. Mules.	Total. Animals.	Quantity Issued. Corn. Pounds.	Quantity Issued. Oats. Pounds.	Quantity Issued. Hay. Pounds.	Quantity Issued. Fodder. Pounds.	Average cost of Corn per bushel, (56 lbs.) $	c.	Oats, per bushel, (32 lbs.) $	c.	Hay, per 100 pounds. $	c.	Fodder per 100 pounds. $	c.	Remarks.
	Field and staff officers, .	6	..	..	12	..	18	6,480	..	1,350	..	1	00		50		50	1	00	Hay purchased at ——, at —— per 100 pounds. Corn purchased at ——, and hauled at —— per bush, Fodder delivered at the post, at —— per 100 lbs.
	Qr. Master's Department,	60	300	80	..	..	440	158,400	..	33,000										
	Total, . . .	219	300	80	26	..	625	225,000	..	38,000	1,640									

I certify, on honor, that the above report is correct

A. B., *Quartermaster.*

No. 7.

Report of Officers of the Army stationed at ——, *whose Quarters and Fuel are commuted, for the month of* —— 186 , *by* ——.

Names.	Rank.	Corps.	Period.		Quarters.					Fuel.							Under what order.	Remarks.
			From.	To.	Room No.	Rate per month.		Amount.		Wood.			Price per cord.		Amount.			
						Dolls.	Cts.	Dolls.	Cts.	Cords.	Feet.	Ins.	Dolls.	Cts.	Dolls.	Cts.		
																		Paid.
							Amount of Quarters, $							Amount of Fuel, $				

I certify, on honor, that the above report is correct.

A. B., *Quartermaster.*

No. 8.

Report of Persons Hired and Employed in the Quartermaster's Department at ——, who have deceased, departed, or have been discharged the service with pay due, during the month of —— 186 , by ——.

No.	Names.	Occupation.	RATE OF PAY OR HIRE.			TIME FOR, AND AMOUNT REMAINING UNPAID.				REMARKS.
			Dolls.	Cts.	Per day or month.	From.	To.	Dolls.	Cts.	
11	George Peters,	Blacksmith,	2	00	Day,	1 Aug. 1860.	30 Sept. 1860,	52	00	Discharged 30th Sep. 1860; certificates given.
27	John Smith,	Teamster,	25	00	Month,	1 Sept. 1860,	15 Sept. 1860,	12	50	Deserted 16th Sept. 1860.
29	Peter Davis,	Laborer,	20	00	Month,	1 Sept. 1860,	15 Sept. 1860,	10	00	Died 24th Sept. 1860.
								$ 75	50	

I certify, on honor, that the above is a true report of all persons hired and employed by me in the Quartermaster's Department, who have deceased, deserted, or been discharged the service with pay due, and that the statement of time for, and amount remaining unpaid, and the remarks are correct and just.

A. B., *Quartermaster.*

NOTE.—This report must contain all the information required, to enable the Department to pay to the legal representatives of the deceased persons, to examine into the case of deserters, and to examine and verify the correctness of payments made on certificates of discharge.

No. 9.

Estimate of Funds required for the service of the Quartermaster's Department at ——, by ——, in the month of ——, 186 .

		Dolls.	Cts.
1	For Fuel, ...		
2	Forage, ...		
3	Straw, ...		
4	Stationery, ...		
5	Materials for building. (State what, and for what,) .		
6	Hire for mechanics. (State for what work,) . .		
7	Hire for laborers. (State for what service,) . .		
8	Hire of teamsters. (State on what service,) . .		
9	Pay of extra-duty men. (State for what work,) .		
10	Pay of wagon and forage masters, ...		
11	Hire of clerks, guides, escorts, expenses of courts-martial, of burials, of apprehending deserters, and other incidental expenses, ...		
12	Hire or commutation of officers' quarters, . .		
13	Hire of quarters for troops, or ground for encampment or use of military stations, ...		
14	Hire of store houses, offices, &c. (For what use,) .		
15	Mileage to officers, ...		
16	Army transportation, viz:		
	Of troops and their baggage, . . .		
	Of Quartermaster's subsistence, ordnance, and hospital stores, ...		
17	Purchase of horses and mules. (Q. M. Dep.) . .		
18	Purchase of wagons and harness. do. . .		
19	Purchase of horses for mounted troops, viz:		
	Horses for Company —— Cavalry, . .		
	Horses for Company —— Artillery, &c., . .		
20	Outstanding Debts,*		
	Deduct actual or probable balance on hand, . .		

* To be accompanied by a list giving the name and amount due each individual, or firm, and on what account due.

No. 10.

The Confederate States in account current with ——, Quartermaster Confederate States. on account of the Quartermaster's Department at ——, in the quarter ending on the —— day of ——, 186 .

Dr. 186 .				186 .		Cr.	
March 31,	To amount of purchases, per abstract A,			January 1	By balance on hand, per last account, -		
" 31,	To amount of expenditures, per abst'ct B,			" 15	By cash received from Treasurer of the Confederate States, being amount of warrant No. ——, - - -		
" 31,	To amount of transfers to officers, per abstract B *b*, - - - -			March 31	By cash received of sundry officers, per abstract B *b b*, - - - -		
" 31,	To balance due the Confederate States, carried to new account, - -			" 31	By cash received from sales of public property, as per account herewith, -		

I certify that the above is a true account of all the moneys that have come into my hands, on account of the Quartermaster's Department, during the quarter ending on the —— day of —— 186 , and that the disbursements have been faithfully made.

A. B., *Quartermaster*.

Note.—Moneys for clothing, camp and garrison equipage, and contingencies of the army, are not accounted for in this account current. **Abstracts B *b* and B *b b* are used only where the number of transfers make them necessary.**

No. 11.—(Abstract A.)

Abstract of Purchases paid for at ——, in the quarter ending on the —— 186 , by ——.

Classes.					Fuel.				Forage.			Straw.	Stationery.													
Date.	No of voucher.	From whom purchased.	Amount.		Wood.			Coal	Corn.	Oats.	Hay.	Pounds.														
			Dolls.	Cents.	Cords.	Feet	Ins.	Lbs.	Bu.	Bu.	Lbs															
Purchased prior to the quarter,																										
Purchased within the quarter,																										
Total paid within the quarter,																										

Note.—This abstract will be supported by vouchers (Form 12), and must exhibit all the articles paid for in the quarter, whether purchased within or prior to the quarter, except purchases of clothing, camp and garrison equipage, and purchases for "army contingencies."

No. 12.—(Voucher for Purchases to Abstract A.)

The Confederate States,

To ——— ———. Dr.

Date of purchase.		Dollars.	Cents.
June 3, 1860, .	20 cords of wood, at ——— per cord, ...		
" 10, " .	20,251 pounds of straw, at ——— per 100 lbs.		
" 29, " .	100 bushels of coal, at ——— per bushel, ...		
	$		

I certify that the above account is correct and just; the articles are to be (or have been) accounted for on my property return for the ——— quarter ending on the —— day of ——— 186 .

A. B., *Quartermaster.*

Received at ———, the —— of ——— 186 , of C. D., Quartermaster C. S. Army, ——— dollars and ——— cents, in full of the above account.

E. F.

(Signed duplicates.)

Note.—The certificate made by the officer who purchased the property. The receipt taken by the officer who paid it.

No. 13.—(Abstract B.)

Abstract of Expenditures on the Quartermaster's Department, by ——, at ——, in the quarter ending on the of —— 186 .

Date of payment.	No. of voucher.	To whom paid.	On what account.	Amount.	
				Dolls.	Cts.
			$		

I certify that the above abstract is correct.

A. B., *Quartermaster.*

Note.—This abstract contains all payments in the account current, except purchases (Abstract) and transfers of funds.

No. 14.—(Abstract B *b*.)

Abstract of Advances made to Officers for Disbursements on account of the Quartermaster's Department, by ——, *in the quarter ending the* ——, 136 .

Date of the advance.	No. of the receipt or voucher.	To what officer.	By whose order, or for what purpose.	Amount.	
				Dolls.	Cts.
			$		

No. 15.(—VOUCHER TO ABSTRACT B.)

We, the subscribers, do hereby acknowledge to have received of ———, Assistant Quartermaster C. S. Army at ———, the sums opposite to our names respectively, being in full of our pay for the period herein expressed, having signed duplicates hereof.

Date.	No.	Names.	Occupation.	Period of service.				Rate of pay.			Amount of pay.		Am't of stop'ges.		Amount rec'd.		Signers' names.	Witnesses.	Remarks.
				From.	To.	Months.	Days.	Dollars.	Cents.	Per month or day.	Dollars.	Cents.	Dollars.	Cents.	Dollars.	Cents.			

I certify, on honor, that the above receipt roll is correct and just.

A. B., *Quartermaster.*

No. 16.—(VOUCHER TO ABSTRACT B.)

The Confederate States,

To ——— ———, DR.

Date.		Dolls.	Cents.
From —— of —— to —— of ——	For mileage from ——— to ———, being ——— miles, at ——— per mile, ...		

I certify, on honor, that the above is correct and just; that I performed the journey, and under the order hereto annexed, and not returning from leave of absence to the station or troops I had left; that I have not been furnished with public transportation, nor received money in lieu thereof, for any part of the route.

Received, ——— 186 , of ———, ——— dollars and ——— cents in full of the above account.

(Signed duplicate.)

No. 17.—(Voucher to Abstract B.)

The Confederate States,

To ——— ———, Dr.

Date.		Dolls.	Cents.
	For expenses incurred for transportation of self and allowance for baggage, and porterage in traveling from ——— to ———, per annexed statement, ...		

I certify, on honor, that the above account is correct and just; that I have performed the journey, and on urgent public duty, without orders, for the purpose of ————, and necessarily incurred the expenses as stated; that I have travelled in the customary reasonable manner, and not returning from leave of absence to the station or troops I left; that I have not been furnished with public transportation, or money in lieu thereof, for any part of the route. The approval of the journey by the proper authority is hereto annexed.

Received at ———, the ——— of ——— 186 , of ————, Assistant Quartermaster C. S. Army, ——— dollars and ——— cents, in full of the above account.

(Signed in duplicate.)

Dolls. $\overline{100}$

Certificate in case of journey under orders.

I certify, on honor, that this account is correct and just; that I performed the journey, and under the order hereto annexed, and necessarily incurred the expenses as stated; that I traveled in the customary reasonable manner; that I was not returning from leave of absence to the station or troops I had left; that I have not been furnished with public transportation, nor money in lieu thereof, for any part of the route.

No. 18.—(Voucher to Abstract B.)

The Confederate States,

To ——— ———, Dr.

Date.		Dolls.	Cents.
	For mileage from ——— to ———, pursuant to annexed copy of Orders No. ———, convening (or annexed summons to attend) a court-martial at ———, distance being ——— miles, at ——— cents per mile, ...		
	——— days' attendance on said court-martial, being from the ——— of ——— to the ——— of ——— 186 , inclusive (per annexed certificate), at $———, ...		
	——— days' traveling on the ——— of ———, going to, and on the ——— of ———, returning from, the court at $———, ...		

I certify, on honor, that the above account is correct and just; that I have actually performed the journeys herein charged for on the days stated. in obedience to the authority hereunto annexed; that I have not been furnished with public transportation, nor received money in lieu thereof, for any part of the route charged for.

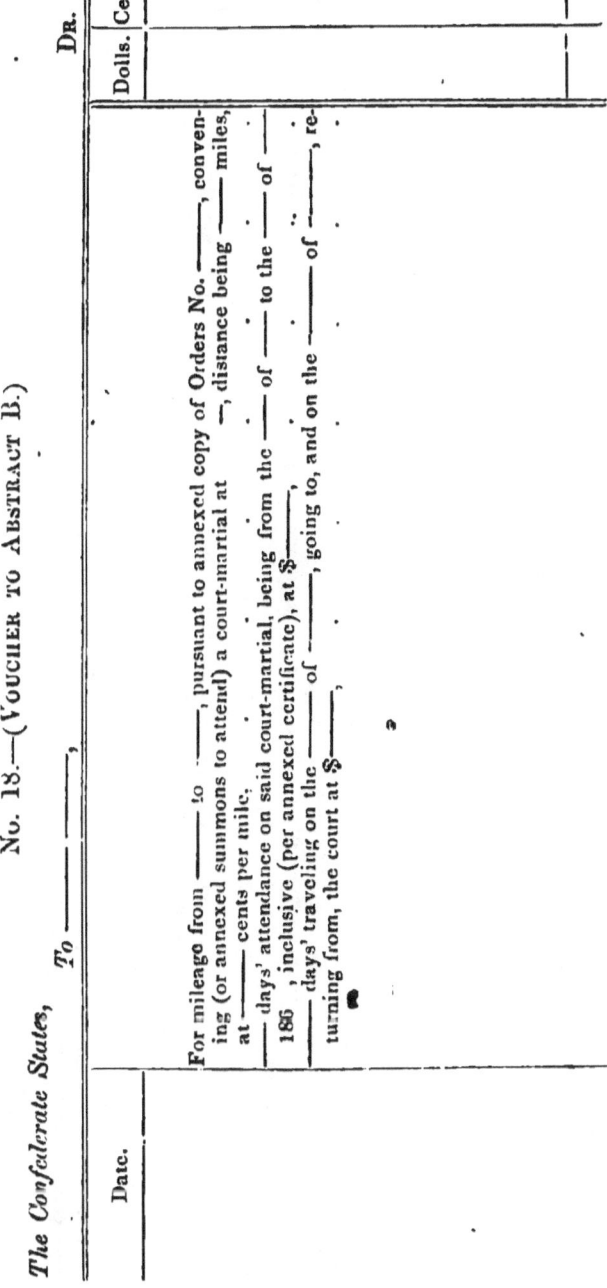

Received at ——— the ——— of ——— 186 , of ———, Assistant Quartermaster C. S. Army, ——— dollars and ——— cents, in full of the above account.

(Signed in duplicate.)

No. 19.—(Voucher to Abstract B.)

The Confederate States,

To ——— ———, Dr.

Date.		Dolls.	Cents.
	For the actual expense of his transportation, while traveling under orders in the discharge of his duty as clerk to Major ———, Paymaster Confederate States Army, from ——— to ———, per annexed statement, ...		

I certify, on honor, that ——— was, during the time above specified, employed as clerk in the Pay Department, Confederate States Army, and that the journey charged for in the above account was performed by him in the discharge of his official duties, under my orders. ——— ———, *Paymaster C. S. Army.*

——— County, *ss.*

On this ——— day of ——— one thousand eight hundred and sixty ———, personally appeared before me, the subscriber, a justice of the peace in and for the county aforesaid, ———, and made oath in due form of law, that the above account is correct and just, and exhibits the actual expense of his transportation for and during the journey above specified.

(Subscribed in duplicate.)

——— ———, *Justice of the Peace.*

Received at ———, the ——— of ——— 186 , of ———, Assistant Quartermaster Confederate States Army, ——— dollars and ——— cents, in full of the above account.

(Signed in duplicate.)

Dollars $\frac{}{100}$

No. 20.—(Voucher to Abstract B.)

The Confederate States,

To —— ——, Dr.

Date.		Dolls.	Cents.
	For cash paid for postage on letters and packages on public service, received and sent by him from the —— of —— 186 , to the —— of —— 186 , inclusive,		

I certify, on honor, that the foregoing account is correct and just; that the letters and packages on which postage has been paid, as therein stated, were all on public service; that I have actually paid the amount charged.

E. F.

Received at ——, the —— of —— 186 , of ——, Assistant Quartermaster C. S. Army, —— dollars and —— cents, in full of the above account.

(Signed in duplicate.)

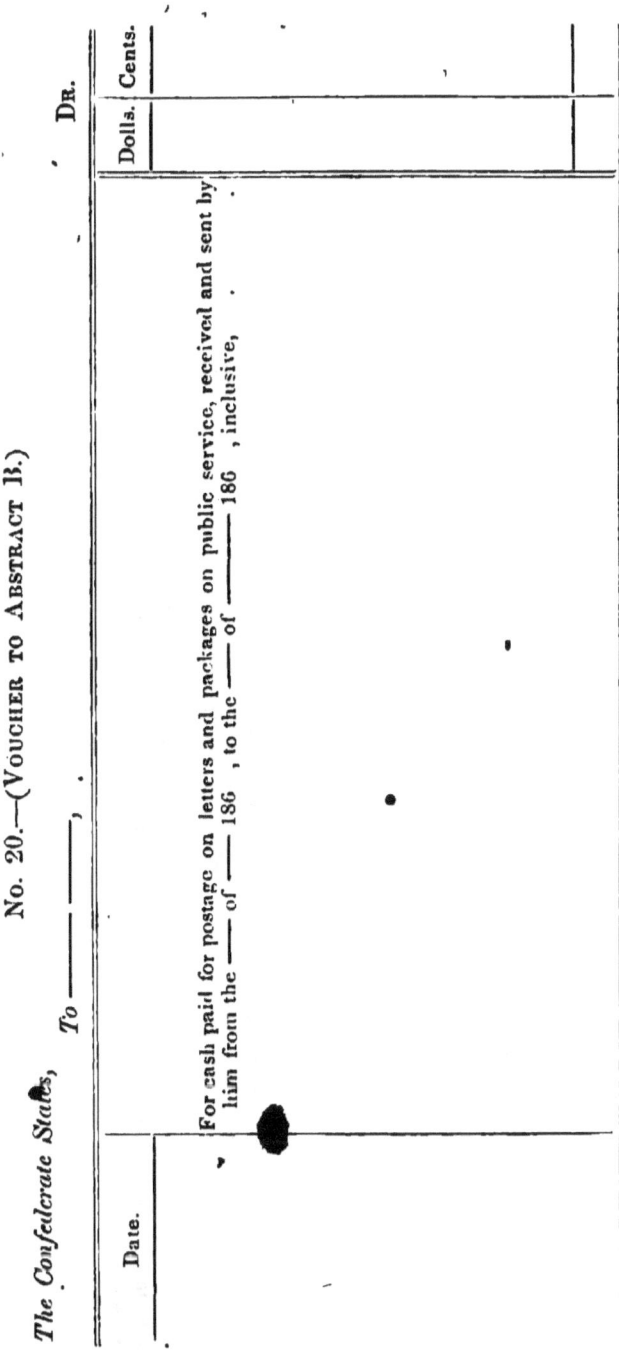

No. 21.—(Voucher to Abstract B.)

The Confederate States,

To —— ——, Dr.

Date.		Dolls.	Cents.
	For commutation of quarters at ——, from the —— of —— 186 , to the —— of —— 186 , inclusive, ...		
	For —— rooms, at —— dollars each, per month, ...		
	For commutation of fuel for the same period:		
	—— cords —— feet —— inches, at —— dollars per cord, .		

I certify, on honor, that there were no quarters owned or hired by the public at the above station which could be assigned to —— during the above period, and that the fuel is charged at the average market price for the month.

A. B., *Quartermaster.*

I certify, on honor, that the above account is correct and just; that I have been regularly stationed on duty at ——, by ——, during the period charged for; that I have not been furnished with quarters, rent, or fuel by the public, nor received a commutation of money in lieu thereof.

C. D.

Received at ———, the —— of —— 186 , of ———, Quartermaster C. S. Army, —— dollars and —— cents, in full of the above account.

(Signed in duplicate.)

C. D.

Note.—The certificate must show by whose order the officer was stationed, and the first account to be accompanied by a copy of the order.

No. 22.—(Voucher.)

The Confederate States,

To —— ——, Dr.

Date.		Dolls.	Cents.

I certify, on honor, that the above account is correct and just; that the services were rendered as stated, and that they were necessary for the public service.

A. B., *Quartermaster.*

Received of —— 186 , of ——, —— dollars and —— cents, in full of the above account.

(Signed duplicates.) E. F.

Note.—This form will be used for miscellaneous disbursements, and will be entered in abstract B or C, according to the nature of the expenditure.

No. 23.

QUARTERLY RETURN OF QUARTERMASTER'S STORES

Received, issued, and remain on hand at ——, in the quarter ending on the —— of —— 186 .

A. B., *Quartermaster.*

NOTE.

The property on this return (which does not include clothing, camp and garrison equipage) will be classed as follows:

1. Fuel.
2. Forage.
3. Straw.
4. Stationery.
5. Barrack, Hospital, and office Furniture.
6. Means of Transportation, including Harness, &c.
7. Building Materials.
8. Veterinary Tools and Horse Medicines.
9. Blacksmiths' Tools.
10. Carpenter's Tools.
11. Wheelwrights' Tools.
12. Mason's and Bricklayers' Tools.
13. Miscellaneous Tools for Fatigue and Garrison purposes.
14. Stores for Expenditure, such as Iron, Steel, Horse-shoes, Rope, &c., &c. to be classed alphabetically.

No. 23.—Quarterly Return of Quartermaster's Stores received and issued
——. Con

Classes,			1 Fuel.				
			Wood.			Coal.	
Date.	Abstracts, &c.		Cords.	Feet.	Inches.	Anthracite.	Bituminous.
			No.	No.	No.	Lbs.	Bu.
	Per last return,	On hand, ...					
	Abstract D,	Received by purchase, .					
	" E, .	" from officers, .					
	" N,	Fabricated, taken up, &c.,					
Total to be accounted for, ...							
	Per Abstract F,	Fuel, ...					
	" G.	Forage, ...					
	" H,	Straw, ...					
	" I.	Stationery, ...					
	" K,	Special issues, . . .					
	" L.	Expended, sold, &c. . .					
	" M,	Transferred, . . .					
Total issued and expended, ...							
Total remaining on hand.							
Condition 1, . .		In good order, ...					
" 2, . .		Unfit for service, but repairable, ...					
" 3, . .		Totally unfit for service. .					

at ——, in the quarter ending on the —— of —— 186 , by
tinued.

2. Forage.				3 Straw.	4. Stationery.						
Corn	Oats.	Hay.	Fodder.	For Bedding.	Foolscap Paper.	Letter Paper.	Folio Post Paper.	Envelope Paper.	Envelopes.	Two qr. blank books.	Three qr. blk. books.
Lbs.	Lbs.	Lbs.	Lbs.	Pounds.	Qrs.	Qrs.	Qrs.	Qrs.	No.	No.	No.

No. 23.—*Quarterly return of Quartermaster's Stores, received and issued*

Con

4. Stationery.

Abstracts, &c.	Four qr. blank books.	Ink.	Ink-powder.	Wafers.	Sealing-wax.	Steel pens.	Quills.	Lead-pencils.	Office tape.	Inkstands.	Wafer-stamps.
	No.	Botls.	Paprs.	Ozs.	Ozs.	No.	Gross.	No.	Pcs.	No.	No.
O H, .											
D, .											
E, .											
N, .											
F, .											
G, .											
H, .											
I, .											
K, .											
L, .											
M, .											

at ——, *in the quarter ending on the* —— *of* —— 186 , *by* ——.
tinued.

4. Stationery.

Erasers.	Paper-folders.	Sand-boxes.	Wafer-boxes.												
No.	No.	No.	No.												

I certify, on honor, that the foregoing return exhibits a true and correct statement of all the property which has come into my hands on account of the Quartermaster's Department, during the quarter ending on the —— of —— 186 .

A. B., *Quartermaster.*

No. 24.—(ABSTRACT D.)

Abstract of Articles purchased at ——, in the quarter ending on the —— 186 , by ——.

CLASSES.					FUEL.				FORAGE.	STRAW.	STATIONERY.		
Date.	No of voucher.	From whom purchased.	Amount.		Wood.			Coal					
			Dols	Cts.	Cords.	Feet	Ins.	Bu.					
Articles purchased and paid for.													
Articles purchased and not paid for.													
Total purchased within the quarter.													

I certify that the above abstract is correct.

A. B., *Quartermaster.*

NOTE.—This abstract appertains exclusively to the *Property Return*, and is designed to show all the supplies purchased by the quartermaster, *whether paid for or not*. No voucher of the purchase paid for accompany this abstract. They are in the second divison of Abstract A. Purchase not paid for are vouched as in Form No. 25.

No. 25.—(Voucher to Abstract D.)

The Confederate States

To ——— ———, Dr.

Date of purchase.		Dolls.	Cents.
	For ——— cords of wood, at ——— per cord, ...		
	For ——— pounds of hay, at ——— per 100 pounds, . . .		

I certify, on honor, that the above account is correct and just; that I purchased the articles above enumerated of the said ——, at the prices therein charged, amounting to —— dollars and cents, and that I have not paid the account. (Here state the cause of non-payment.)

A. B., *Quartermaster.*

No. 26.—(Abstract E.)

Abstract of Articles received from officers at ———, *in the quarter ending on* —— *of* —— 186 , *by* ——.

Classes.			Fuel.				Forage.			Straw.			Stationery.																	
			Wood.			Coal.																								
Date.	No. of voucher.	From whom rec'ved.	Cords	Feet.	Inches.	Bushels.																								
Total received,																														

I certify that the above abstract is correct.

A. B., *Quartermaster*.

Note.—All property received from other officers will be entered on this abstract, whether receipted for or not. For voucher, see Form No. 27.

No. 27.—(Voucher to Abstract E.)

List of Quartermaster's Stores, &c., delivered by —— to ——, at ——, on the —— day of —— 186 .

Number or quantity.		Articles.	Cost when new.	Condition when delivered.	Remarks.
40	Forty,	Felling axes,	$ 1 00 each,	New,	
300	Three hundred pounds,	Bar iron, assorted,	6 per pound,	New,	
1,000	One thousand pounds,	Cut nails,	5 per pound,	New,	
656	Six hundred and fifty-six bushels,	Corn,	1 00 per bushel,	Good,	
30,500	Thirty thousand five hundred lbs,	Hay,	1 00 per hundred,	Good,	
10	Ten,	Wheelbarrows,	4 00 each,	Half-worn,	
5	Five,	Wagons (4-horse,)	150 00 each,	Half-worn,	
5	Five,	Wagous "	150 00 each,	New,	

I certify that I have this day delivered to A. B., Quartermaster Confederate States Army, the articles specified in the foregoing list.

C. D., *Quartermaster.*

Note.—When no invoice is received, the receiving officer will substitute for this form of voucher a list of the stores received, certified by himself. When the person responsible for the property entered without invoice is known, it will be entered in his name.

No 28.—(Abstract F.)

Abstract of Fuel issued at ——, *in the quarter ending on the* —— *of* —— 186 , *by* ——.

Date.	No. of voucher.	To whom issued.	For what period.	Wood.			Coal.		Remarks.
				Cords.	Feet.	Inches.	Bushels.	Pounds.	
Total issued, ...									

I certify that the abstract is correct.

A. B., *Quartermaster.*

Note.—For vouchers, see Forms No. 29 and No. 30. All fuel issued is entered on this abstract. Fuel transferred to other officers, to be accounted for by them, is entered on abstract M.

No. 29.—(VOUCHER TO ABSTRACT F.)

Requisition for Fuel for —— *Company* —— *Regiment of* ——, *commanded by* ——, *for the month of* —— 186 .

STATION.	Captains.	Subalterns.	Non-commissioned officers, musicians and privates.	Laundresses.	Total.	Monthly allowance to each, in cords	TOTAL ALLOWANCE.					Remarks.
							Wood.			Coal.		
							Cords.	Feet.	Inches.	Bush.	Pounds.	
Total. . . .												

I certify, on honor, that the above requisition is correct and just; and that fuel has not been drawn for any part of the time above charged.

R. S., *Commanding Company.*

Received, —— 186 , of ——, Assistant Quartermaster C. S. Army, —— cords —— feet —— inches of wood and —— of coal, in full of the above requisition.

(Signed duplicates.)

R. S. *Commanding Company.*

No. 30.—(Voucher to Abstract F.)

Requisition for Fuel for ——, stationed at ——, for the month of —— 186 .

				WOOD.			COAL.		REMARKS.
				Cords.	Feet.	Inches.	Bushels.	Pounds.	
For myself, . . .									
Total, ...									

I certify, on honor, that the above requisition is correct and just, and that I have not drawn fuel for any part of the time above charged.

Received, —— 186 , of ——, Assistant Quartermaster Confederate States Army, —— cords —— feet —— inches of wood and —— of coal, in full of the above requisition.

Note—This form will be used for individual officers, hospitals, guards, &c.

No[illegible]—(ABSTRACT G.)

Abstract of Forage issued at ——, *in the quarter ending on the* —— *of* —— 186 , *by* ——.

Date.	No of voucher.	To whom issued.	For what period.		Number of horses.	Number of mules.	Number of oxen.	Total.	Total allowance.						Remarks.
									Corn.		Oats.		Hay.	Fodder.	
			From.	To.					Bushels. (56 lbs.)	Pounds.	Bushels. (32 lbs.)	Pounds.	Pounds.	Pounds.	
															Public. Private.
	Total, ...														

I certify that the above abstract is correct. A. B., *Quartermaster.*

NOTE.—For vouchers, see Forms Nos. 32, 33, 34. All forage issued will be entered on this abstract. Forage transferred to other officers, to be accounted for by them, will be entered on abstract M.

No. 32.—(Voucher to Abstract G.)

Requisition for Forage for Public Horses, Mules and Oxen, in the service of ——, for —— days, commencing the —— of —— 186 , at ——.

Date of requisition.	Number of horses.	Number of mules.	Number of Oxen.	Total number of animals.	Number of days.	Number of rations.	Daily allowance to each animal.					Total allowance.					Remarks.
							Pounds of corn.	Pounds of barley.	Pounds of oats.	Pounds of hay.	Pounds of fodder.	Corn. Pounds of.	Barley. Pounds of.	Oats. Pounds of.	Hay. Pounds of.	Fodder. Pounds of.	
Required, . . . On hand, to be deducted, .																	
To be supplied, . . .																	

I certify, on honor that the above requisition is correct and just; that I have now in service the number of animals for which forage is required; and that forage has not been received for any part of the time specified.

Received at ——. on the —— day of —— 186 , of ——, Quartermaster C. S. Army, —— pounds of corn, —— pounds of barley, —— pounds of oats, —— pounds of hay, —— pounds fodder, in full of the above requisition.

(Signed in duplicate.)

No. 33.—(Voucher to Abstract G.)

Requisition for Forage for —— *Private Horses in the service of* ——, *C. S. Army, at* ——, *for* —— *days, commencing the* —— *of* ——, *and ending the* —— *of* —— 186 .

Date.	Period.		Number of horses.	Daily allowance for each.			Total allowance.						Remarks.
	From.	To.		Corn.	Oats.	Hay.	Corn.		Oats.		Hay.	Fodder.	
				Pounds.	Pounds.	Pounds.	Bushels. (52 lbs.)	Pounds.	Bushels, (32 lbs.)	Pounds.	Pounds.	Pounds.	
Total,													

I certify, on honor, that the above requisition is correct and just; and that I have not drawn forage for any part of the time above charged.

Received at ——, the —— of —— 186 , of ——, Assistant Quartermaster C. S. Army, —— —/56 bushels corn, —— —/32 bushels oats, —— pounds hay, —— pounds fodder, in full of the above requisition.

(Signed duplicates.)

No. 34.—(VOUCHER TO ABSTRACT G.)

Statement of Forage issued to and consumed by the Public Animals under my direction at ———, *during the month of* ——— 186 .

Period.			Number of animals.				Total allowance.						Remarks.
							Corn.	Oats.	Barley	Hay.	Fodder.		
From.	To.	No. of days.	Horses.	Mules.	Oxen.	Total.	Pounds of.	Pounds of.	Pounds of.	Pounds of.	Pounds of.		
Total,													

I certify, on honor, that the above statement is correct; that the forage was issued to the Public Animals as stated, and that the issues were necessary.

A. B., *Quartermaster.*

Approved: R. S., *Commanding.*

No. 35.—(Abstract H.)

Abstract of Straw issued at ——, *in the quarter ending on the* —— *of* —— 186 , *by* ——.

Date.	No of voucher.	To whom issued.	For what period.		Non-commissioned officers, musicians, and privates.	Laundress.	Hospital.	Total allowance.	Remarks.
			From.	To.				Pounds.	
		Total.							

I certify that the above abstract is correct.

A. B., *Quartermaster.*

Note.—For voucher, see Form 36. Issues on this abstract. Transfers on abstract M.

No. 36.—(Voucher to Abstract H.)

Requisition for Straw for —— *Company* —— *Regiment of* ——, *commanded by* ——, *for the month of* —— 186 .

Station.	Non-commissioned officers, musicians, and privates.	Laundress.	Total drawn for.	Monthly allowance to each.	Total allowance.	Remarks.
				Pounds.	Pounds.	
Total,						

I certify, on honor, that the above return is correct and just; and that straw has not been drawn for any part of the time above charged.

G. H., *Commanding Company.*

Received at ——, the —— of —— 18 , of —— C. S. Army, —— pounds of straw, in full of the above requisition.

(Signed duplicates.)

G. H., *Commanding Company.*

No. 37.—(Abstract I)

Abstract of Stationery issued at ——, *in the quarter ending on the* —— *of* —— 186 , *by* ——.

Date.	No. of voucher.	To whom issued.	For what period.		Writing paper, quires.	Cartridge paper, sheets.	Quills, number.	Wafers, ounces.	Sealing-wax, ounces.	Ink-powder, papers.	Blank books, number.				Remarks.
			From.	To.											
Total issued.															

I certify, that the above abstract is correct.

A. B., *Quartermaster.*

Note.—For voucher, see Form No. 38. The stationery used by the Quartermaster in the public service is entered on this abstract, and all issues by him. Transfers on abstract M.

No. 38.—(Voucher to Abstract I.)

Requisition for Stationery for ——, *stationed at* ——, *for the* ——, *commencing on the* —— *of* ——, *and ending on the* —— *of* —— 186 .

	Quires of letter paper.	Quires of foolscap, paper.	Sheets of cartridge paper.	Number of quills.	Ounces of wafers.	Ounces of sealing wax.	Pieces of tape.	Papers of ink-powder.							

I certify that the above requisition is correct and that I have not drawn stationery for any part of the time specified.

Received at ——, on the —— of —— 186 , of ——, Assistant Quartermaster C. S. Army, —— quires of letter paper, —— quires of foolscap paper, —— quills, —— ounces of wafers, —— ounces of sealing-wax, —— pieces of tape, —— sheets of cartridge paper, —— papers of ink-powder.

(Signed duplicate.)

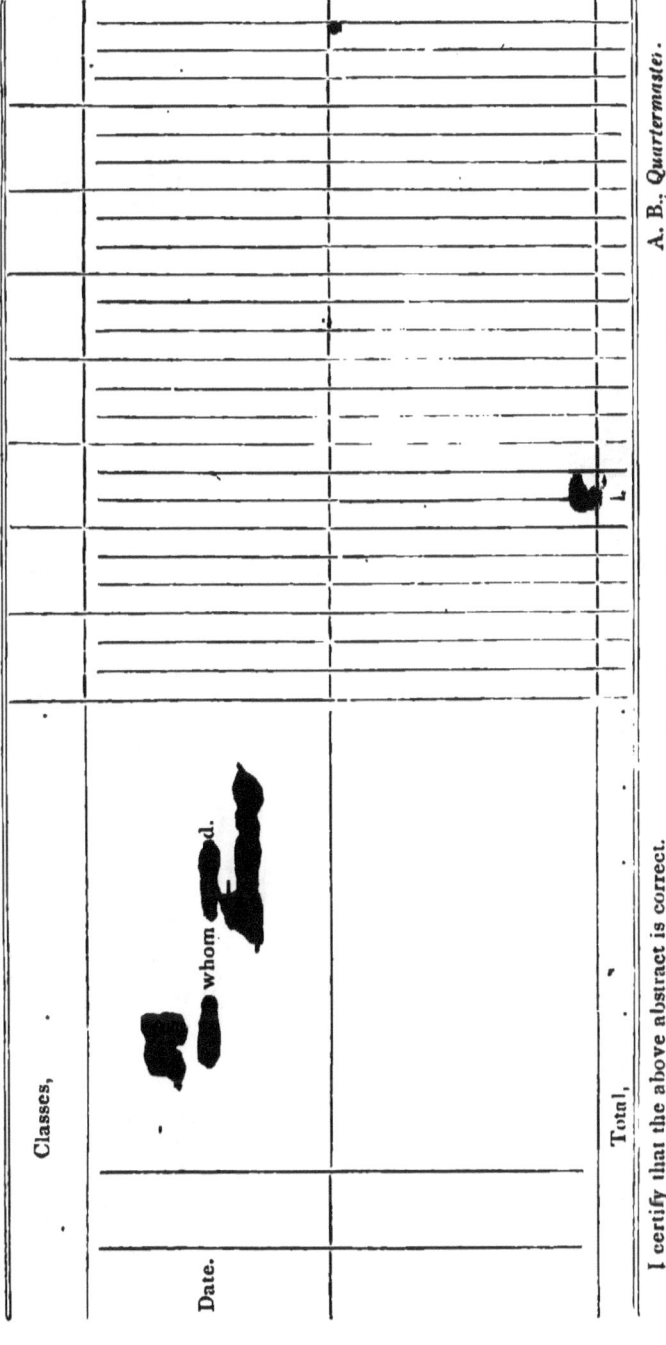

No. 39.—Abstract K.—For all issues except Fuel, Forage, Straw, and Stationery.

Abstract of Articles issued on Special Requisitions at ——, in the quarter ending on the —— of —— 18 , by ——.

Date.			[redacted] [redacted] whom [redacted]d. [redacted]	Classes,							
Total,											

I certify that the above abstract is correct.

A. B., *Quartermaster.*

NOTE.—For voucher see Form No. 10. Transfers on abstract M.

No. 40.—(Voucher to Abstract K.)

SPECIAL REQUISITION.

For

I certify that the above requisition is correct, and that the articles specified are absolutely requisite for the public service, rendered so by the following circumstances: [here the officer will insert such reasons as he may think fit to give, tending to show the necessity for the supplies.]

Captain J. B., Assistant Quartermaster Confederate States Army, will issue the articles specified in the above requisition.

C. D., *Commanding.*

Received at ——, the —— of —— 18 , of ——, Assistant Quartermaster Confederate States Army [here insert the articles,] in full of the above requisition.

(Signed duplicates.)

Note.—The cost of articles issued on special requisitions, and orders of commanding officers, will be entered on the requisition and on the list or invoice furnished the receiving officer.

No. 41.—(Abstract L.)

Abstract of Articles Expended, Lost, Destroyed in the public service, sold, &c., at ———, under the direction of ———, in the quarter ending on the ——— of ——— 186 .

Classes,																	
Date.	No. of certificates.	By whom made.															
Total,																	

I certify that the above abstract is correct.

A. B., *Quartermaster.*

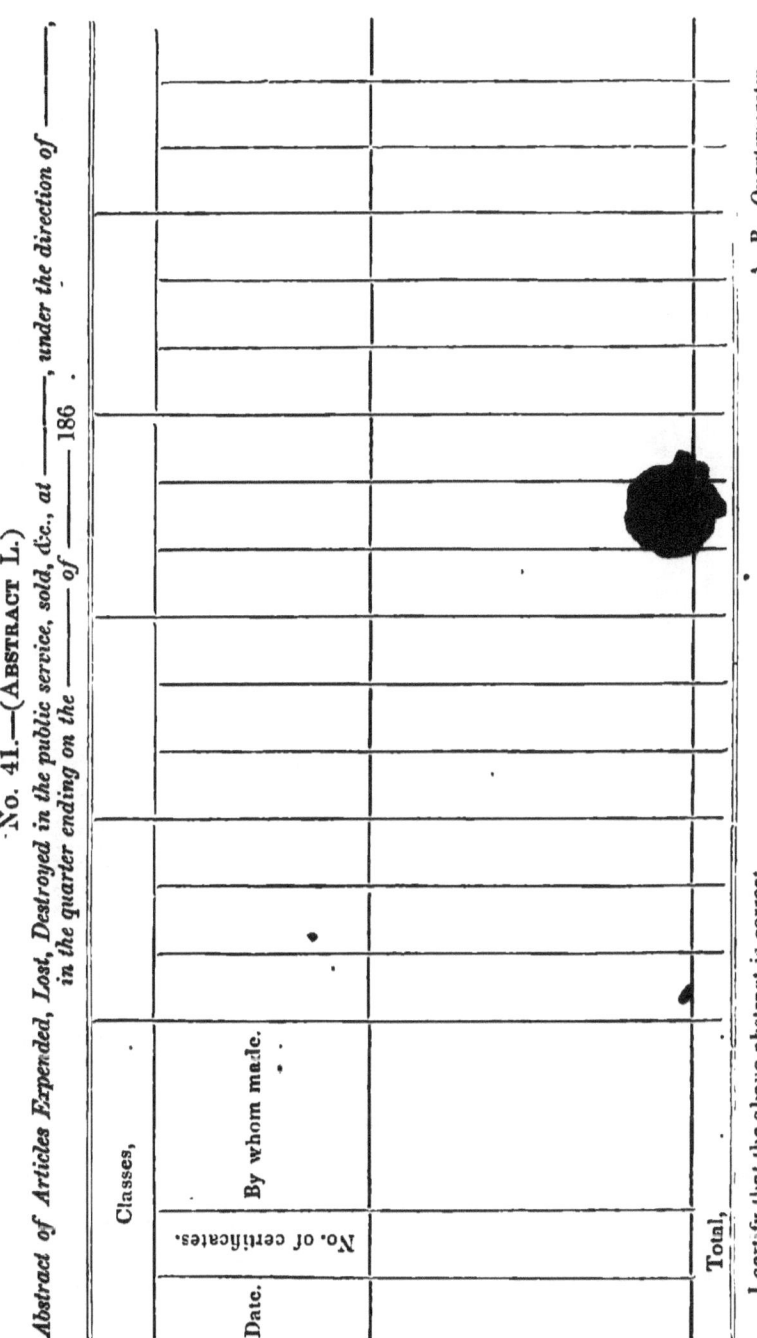

No. 42.—(Voucher to Abstract L.)

List of Quartermaster Stores expended in public service at ——, under the direction of ——, in the month of —— 186 .

No. or quantity.	Articles.	Application.

I certify, on honor, that the several articles of Quartermaster's stores, above examined, have been necessarily expended in the public service at this station, as indicated by the marginal remarks annexed to them respectively.

(Signed duplicates.) A. B., *Quartermaster.*

Note.—This list should be made out monthly, to enable the Quertermaster to know the exact state of his supplies.

No. 43.—(Voucher to Abstract L.)

List of Articles Lost or Destroyed in the public service at ——, *while in the possession and charge of* ——, *in the month of* —— 186 .

No. or quantity.	Articles.	Circumstance and Cause.

I certify that the several articles of Quartermaster's stores, above en[illegible] have been unavoidably lost or destroyed while in the public service, as indicated by the remarks annexed to them respectively.

A. B., *Quartermaster.*

Approved: C. D., *Commanding.*

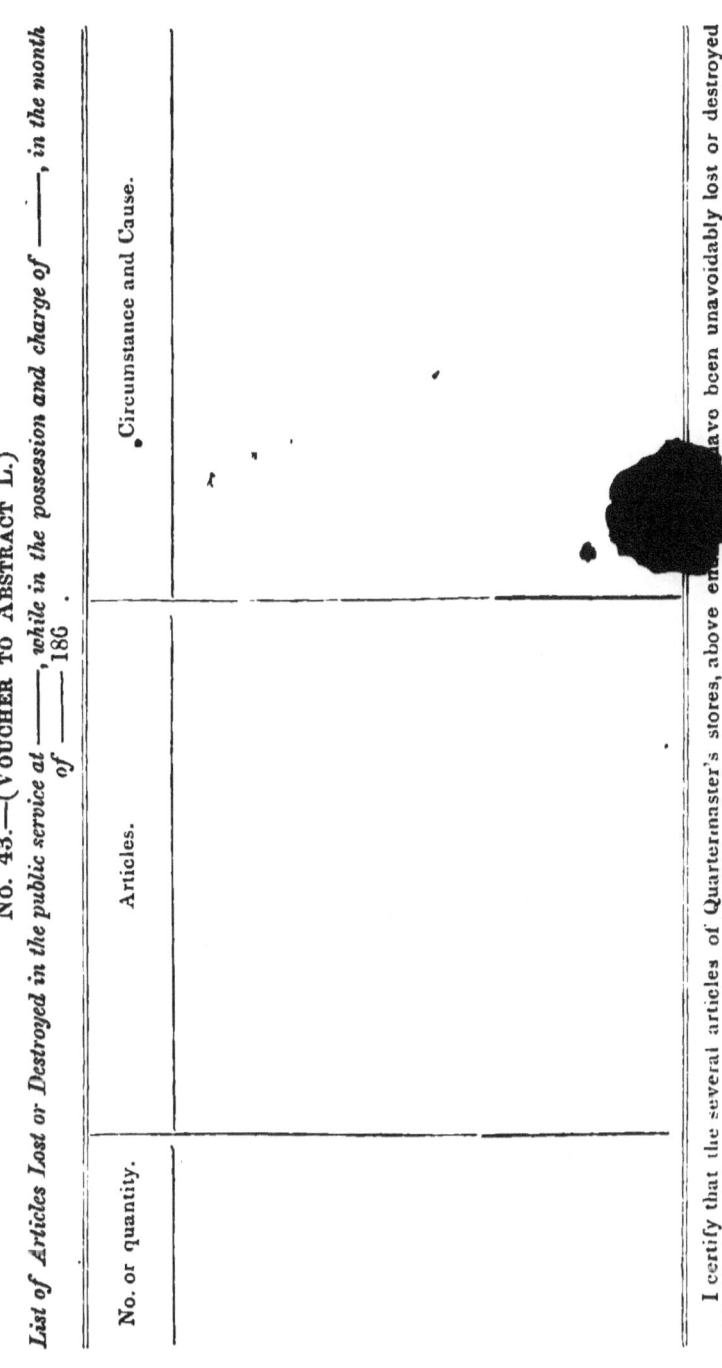

No. 44.—(Voucher to Abstract L.)

Abstract Sales of articles of public property sold at auction at ——— [illegible] *the direction of* ——— *on the* ——— *of* ——— 186[illegible]

No. or quantity.	Articles.	[illegible]	Amount.
			$

I certify that the above account sales is accurate and just.

A. B., *Auctioneer.*

I certify that the above enumerated articles were sold at public auction as above stated, pursuant to—[state the orders or authority.]

C. D., *Quartermaster.*

No. 45.—(Abstract M.)

Abstract of Articles transferred to ——, *at* ——, *in the quarter ending on the* —— *of* —— 186 , *by* ——.

Classes,																		
Date.	No. of voucher.	To whom transferred.																
Total,																		

I certify that the above abstract is correct.

A. B., *Quartermaster.*

Note.—This abstract contains all transfers of stores to other officers, to [illegible]nted for by them; the vouchers will be their receipts. When these are not received in time, the Quartermaster will substitute his own certified list of the stores sent, and the bill of lading. The receipts he will afterwards transmit when he receives them.

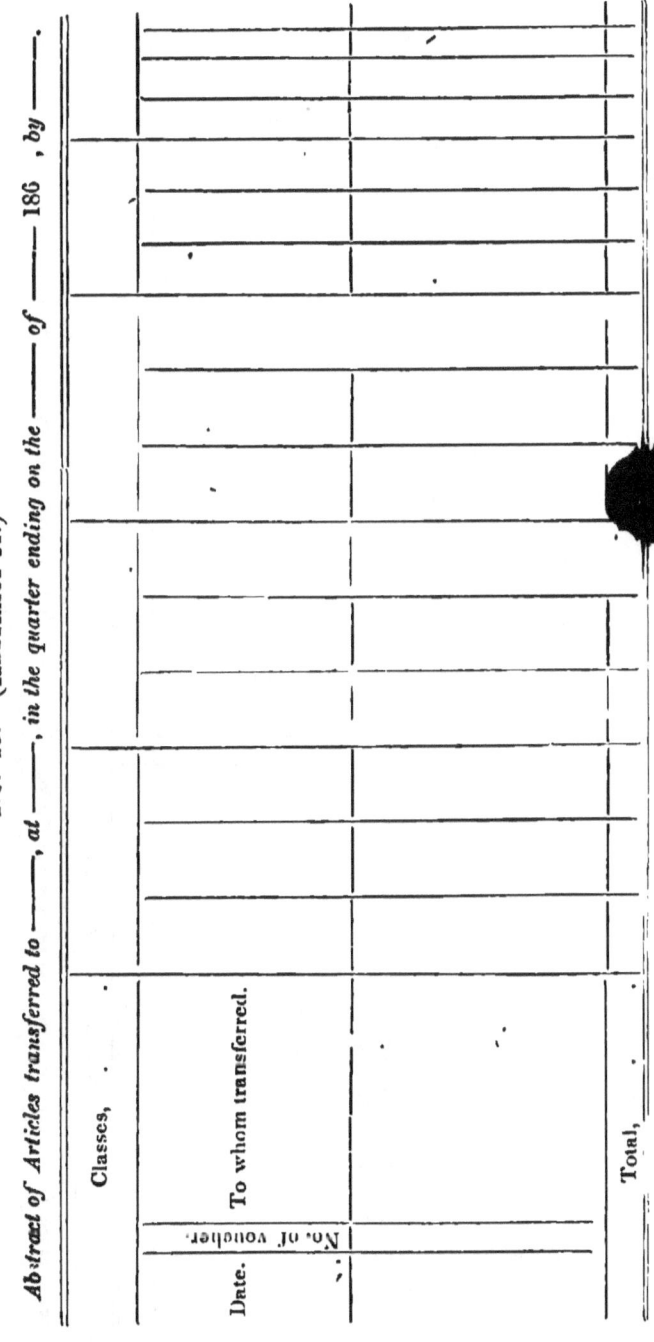

No. 45.—(Abstract N.)

Abstract of Articles received at ——, *during the quarter endi*[illegible] —— *day of* —— 186 .

Classes,			Fuel.				[illegible]			Straw.	Stationery.
			Wood.			Coal.	Corn.	Oats.	Hay.		
Date.	No. of invoice, &c.	From whence received.	Cords.	Feet.	Inches.		Bushels, (35 lbs.)	Bushels. (32 lbs.	Pounds.		
		Found at the post,									
		Manufactured,									
		Parts of articles broken up,									
		Heretofore issued, but not consumed,									
		Captured from the enemy,									
		Total,									

I certify that the above abstract is correct.

A. B., *Quartermaster.*

Note.—This abstract contains all Quartermaster's property found at the post, not borne on the previous return; all that may come to the Quartermaster's possession without his knowing who may be accountable for it; articles manufactured in the quarter; material or parts of articles that have been condemned or broken up; fuel or forage issued but not consumed, &c., &c. Separate lists of each class, with the necessary explanation, will be filled with the abstract.

No. 46.

Quarterly Statement of Allowances paid to Officers of the Army in money, the quarter end

Officers' names.	Rank and Corps. (Rank being that for which they were paid, or allowances furnished.)	For Fuel.		Quarters.			
				In money.		In kind.	
		Period.	Am't $ c.	Period.	$ c.	Period.	No. Rooms.
		1861.		1861.		1861.	
W. S.	Major Genl.	July, Aug. Sep.	96 00	J'ly, Aug. Sep.	120 00	–	–
J. T.	Brig. Genl.	July, . .	30 00	J'ly, Aug. Sep.	80 00	–	–
K. J.	Col. Ajt. Gl.	August, .	30 00	J'ly, Aug. Sep.	90 00	–	–
T. M.	Col. Q. M. D.	August, .	30 00	J'ly, Aug. Sep.	80 00	–	–
T. L.	Maj. Pay Dt.	July. Aug. Sep.	30 00	Aug. Sep.	80 00	July, .	3
L. B.	Col Engrs.	July, Aug. Sep.	39 00	–	80 00	–	–
B. L.	Mj. T. Engrs.	–	–	–	–	–	–
B. B. M.	Cols. Drags.	–	–	–	–	July, Aug.	4
J. C.	Col. Art.	July, Aug. .	20 00	–	–	July, Aug.	4
F. E.	Maj, Infty.	July, Aug. .	12 00	–	–	July, Aug.	4

No. 46.

or furnished in kind, with the money value thereof, by ——, *at* ——, *in*
ing —— 186 .

Rent.	For transportation of baggage.	Per diem on court-martial	For forage issued in kind.	Stationery.	Total Amount.	Abstract and voucher.	Remarks.
$ c.	$ c.	$ c.	$ c.	$ c.	$ c.		
-	120 00	40 00	-	20 00	396 00	B 1, 7, 9—19	
-	90 00	-	-	15 70	215 00	B 2, 11, 14—14	
-	-	-	-	-	120 00	B 17	
-	-	-	-	-	110 00	B 21	
30 00	60 00	-	30 00	-	230 00	B 4, 20—G 13	
-	-	-	-	-	130 00	B 19	
-	100 00	-	-	-	110 00	B 26, 27	
30 00	30 00	40 00	37 50	-	139 50	B 27, 30—G 14	
35 00	70 00	-	-	-	126 50	B 28, 32—H 2	
-	-	-	-	-	12 50	F 4—H 6, .	Public quarters.

I certify that the above is correct. A. B., *Quartermaster.*

NOTE—When officers occupy quarters owned by the public, the number of rooms only will be reported.

No. 47.

The Confederate States in account current with ——, for expenditures on account of Contingencies of the Army and of the other Departments, in the quarter ending on the —— day of ——, 186 .

Date.		Dolls.	Cents.	Date.		Dols	Cts.
Sept. 30,	To amount of expenditures, per Abstract C,			July 1,	By balance on hand, as per last account,		
					By cash received of ——, . .		
Sept. 30,	To balance due the Confederate States, carried to new account, . .			July, 8, Aug. 4,	By cash received from the Treasurer of the Confederate States, being amount of Warrant No. ——, . .		
	$				$		

... the above exhibits a true account of all moneys which have come into my hands on account of contingencies of the army, during the quarter ending on the —— of 186 , and that the disbursements have been faithfully made.

A. B., *Quartermaster.*

No. 48.—(Abstract C.)

Abstract of Disbursements on account of Contingencies of the Army and of other Departments, by ——, in the quarter ending on the —— of —— 186 , at ——.

Date of payment	No. of voucher.	To whom paid.	On what account.	Amount.	
				Dollars.	Cts.

A. B., *Quartermaster.*

Note.—For vouchers, see Forms ——. All payments for apprehending deserters must also be entered in this Abstract.

6

No. 49.—(Voucher to Abstract C.)

Requisition on the Quartermaster's Department for extra supplies of Medicines and Hospital Stores.

I certify, on honor, that the medicines and hospital stores above required are necessary for the use of the sick at this post, in consequence of [here insert whether from loss, damage, &c.,] and that the requisition is agreeable to the supply table.

A. B., *Assistant Surgeon.*

Approved: C. D., *Commanding Officer*,

Received at ——, on the —— of —— 18 , the articles above enumerated.

(Signed duplicates.)

A. B, ***Assistant Surgeon.***

No. 50.—(Voucher to Abstract C.)

Bill of Medicine, &c., when purchased by an officer of the Quartermaster's Department.

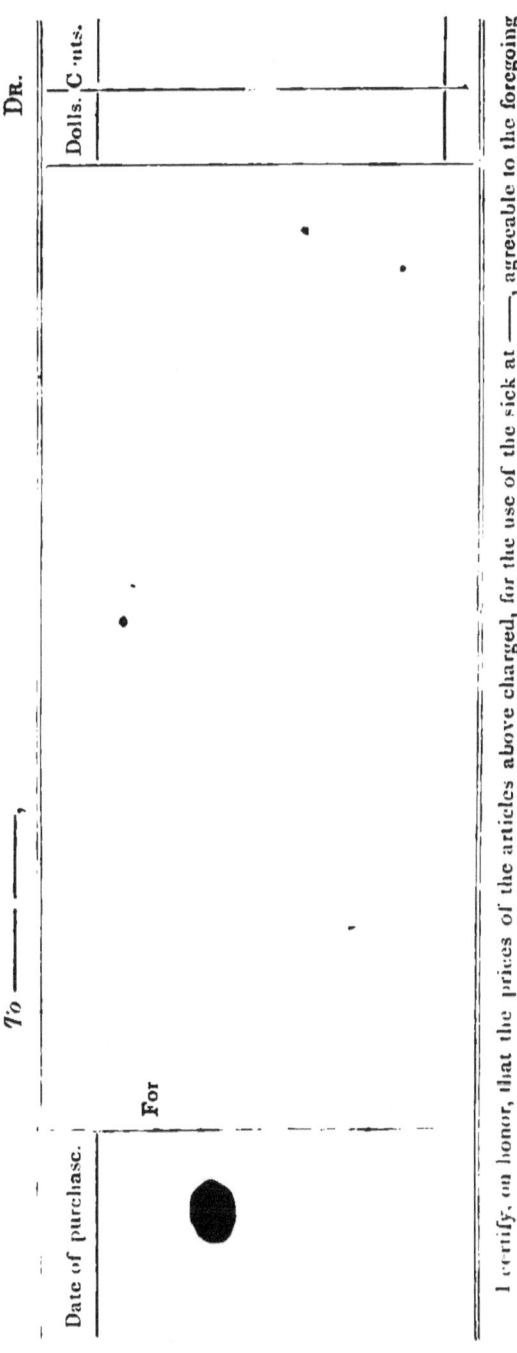

The Confederate States,

To —— ——, DR.

Date of purchase.		Dolls.	Cents.
	For		

I certify, on honor, that the prices of the articles above charged, for the use of the sick at ——, agreeable to the foregoing requisition, are reasonable and just.

A. B., *Surgeon.*

Received of —— 186 , of ——, —— dollars and —— cents, in full of the above account.

(Signed duplicates.) E. F.

Note.—The above certificate may be signed by the surgeon making the requisition, or by any surgeon or assistant surgeon belonging to the army. The requisition on which the purchase may be made must be attached to the bill of purchase, which will be entered in Abstract C, and the articles are noticed in the property returns.

No. 51.—*Quarterly Return of Clothing, Camp and Garrison Equi-*
day of ———

WHEN RECEIVED.	No. of invoice.	OR WHOM RECEIVED.	Cavalry hats.	Caps and bands.	Cap letters, castle, shell and flamd.	Cap covers.	Pompons.	
							Color.	
		On hand per last return.						
Total to be accounted for.								
WHEN ISSUED.	No. of roll.	TO WHOM ISSUED.						
Total issued,								
On hand to be accounted for,								

page, received and issued at ——, in the quarter ending on the ——
186 , *by* ——.

CLOTHING.														
		COATS.									METALLIC SEALS			
Eagle and rings.	Plumes for cavalry.	Sergeant-majors'.	Quartermaster Sergeants'.	Ordnance Sergeants.	Chief musicians'.	First sergeants'.	Sergeants'.	Corporals'.	Musicians.	Privates.	Non-commission-ed officers.	Sergeants'.	Corporals and privates'.	Sashes.

No. 51.—*Quarterly Returns of Clothing, Camp and Garrison*

CLOTHING.														
UNIFORM JACKETS.														
Sergeant-majors'.	Quartermaster Sergeants'.	First sergeants'.	Sergeants'.	Corporals'.	Privates'.	Trowsers.	Yards of binding.		Flannel shirts.	Drawers, parts of.	Boots, cavalry, pairs of.	Boots, infantry, pairs of.	Stockings, pairs of.	Leather stocks.

Equipage, received and issued, &c.—Continued.

CLOTHING.								EQUIPAGE.							
								BED SACKS.							
Great-coats.	Great-coat straps, number of.	Talmas.	Blankets.					Single.	Double.	Axes.	Axe-helves.	Spades.	Camp kettles.	Mess pans.

No. 51.—*Quarterly Return of Clothing, Camp and Gar-*

EQUIPAGE.

Camp hatchets.	Hatchet handles.	Hatchet handles.	Garrison flags.	Garrison flag halliards.	Storm flag.	Recruiting flags.	Recruiting flag halliadrs.	Camp colors.	Guidons.	Trumpets.	Bugles, with extra mouth pieces.	Fifes.	DRUMS.	
													Complete.	Heads, batter.

rison Equipage, received and issued, &c.—Continued.

EQUIPAGE.																									
DRUMS.																				BOOKS AND BLANKS.					
Heads, snare.	Slings.	Sticks, pairs.	Drum-stick carriages.	Cords.	Snares, sets.	Wall-tents.	Wall-tent flies.	Wall-tent poles and pins, sets.	Common tents.	Common tent poles and pins, sets.	Iron pots.	Pickaxes.	Pickaxe handles.							Clothing account book.	Descriptive book	Order book.	Clothing returns.	Receipt rolls.	Final statements

No. 52.

We, the undersigned, Non-Commissioned Officers, Artificers, Musicians,
——— *the several articles of Clothing*

Date of the issue.	Name and designation of the soldier.	Caps.	Cap covers.	Pompons.	Eagles and rings.	UNIFORM COATS.					UNIFORM JACKETS.				
						N. C. S.	Sergeants'.	Corporals'.	Musicians'.	Privates'.	Sergeants'.	Corporals'.	Musicians'.	Privates'.	

NOTES.—Erasures and alterations of entries are prohibited.
Regular and extra issues will be distinguished on the receipt-roll.
Each signature, whether written by the soldier or acknowledged *by mark*, must be witnessed.
Vacant space will be filled by a cipher.
Mounted men may receive *one* pair of "boots" and *two* pairs of "bootees," instead of *four* pairs of bootees.

No. 52.

and Privates of ——, do hereby acknowledge to have received of set opposite our respective names.

Trowsers, pairs.	Flannel shirts.	Drawers, pairs.	Boots, cavalry, pairs.	Bootees, infantry pairs.	Stockings, pairs.	Leather stocks.	Great coats.	Fatigue overalls.	Stable frocks.	Blankets.							Signatures.	Witness.

As the metallic shoulder scales, letters, numbers, castles, and shells and flames will last for many years, they will be borne on the returns as company property in the same manner as are sashes, and other articles of camp and garrison equipage, and will be charged to the soldier only when lost or destroyed through neglect.

No. 53.

Descriptive List of Persons and Articles employed and hired in the Quartermaster's Department, and transferred by ——, at ——, to ——. Quartermaster at ——. on the —— day of —— 186 .

Number of each class.	Articles and names of persons.	Designation and occupation.	Period for which pay is due.				Rate of hire or compensation.			Amount due.		Date of contract, agreement, or entry into service.	By whom owned and where.	Remarks.
			From.	To.	Month.	Days.	Dollars.	Cents.	Month, day or voyage.	Dollars.	Cents.			
	Total amount due,													

I certify, on honor, that the above is a true list of persons and articles transferred by me to ——, at ——, on the —— day of —— 186 ; and that the periods of service, rates of hire or compensation, and amounts due, are correctly stated.

PAY DEPARTMENT.

PAY DEPARTMENT.

1. The troops will be paid in such manner that the arrears shall at no time exceed two months, unless the circumstances of the case render it unavoidable, which the quartermaster charged with the payment shall promptly report to the quartermaster-general.

2. The quartermaster-general shall take care, by timely remittances, that the quartermasters have the necessary funds to pay the troops, and shall notify the remittances to the quartermasters and commanding officers of the respective pay districts.

3. The payments, except to officers and discharged soldiers, shall be made on muster and pay-rolls; those of companies and detachments, signed by the company or detachment commander; of the hospital, signed by the surgeon; and all muster and pay-rolls, signed by the mustering and inspecting officer.

4. When a company is paraded for payment, the officer in command of it shall attend at the pay-table.

5. When a receipt on a pay-roll or account is not signed by the hand of the party, the payment must be witnessed. The witness to be a commissioned officer when practicable.

6. Officers are paid on certified accounts, as in Form 4; discharged soldiers, on accounts according to Form 6, and certificates, Form 5. An officer retiring from service must make affidavit to his pay account, and to the certificate annexed to it, and state his place of residence, and the date when his resignation or removal takes effect. Pay accounts of post chaplains are to be certified by the commanding officer of the post.

7. When an officer is dismissed from the service, he shall not be entitled to pay beyond the day on which the order announcing his dismissal is received at the post where he may be stationed, unless a particular day beyond the time is mentioned in the order.

8. No officer shall receive pay for two staff appointments for the same time.

9. Officers are entitled to pay from the date of the acceptance of their appointments, and from the date of promotion.

10. No account of a restored officer for time he was out of service can be paid, without order of the War Department.

11. As far as practicable, officers are to draw their pay from the quartermaster of the district where they may be on duty.

12. No officer shall pass away or transfer his pay account not actually due at the time; and when an officer transfers his pay account he shall report the fact to the quartermaster-general, and to the quartermaster expected to pay it.

13. No person in the military service, while in arrears to the Confederate States, shall draw pay. When the Secretary of War shall find by report of the Comptroller of the Treasury, or otherwise, that an officer of the army is in arrears to the Confederate States, the quartermaster-general shall be directed to stop his pay to the amount of such arrears, by giving notice thereof to the quartermasters of the army, and to the officer, who may pay over the amount to any quartermaster. And no quartermaster shall make to him any payment on account of *pay*, until he exhibits evidence of having refunded the amount of the arrears, or that his pay accrued and stopped is equal to it, or until the stoppage is removed by the quartermaster-general.

14. No officer or soldier shall receive pay or allowances for any time during which he was absent without leave, unless a satisfactory excuse for such absence be rendered to his commanding officer, evidence of which, in case of an officer, shall be annexed to his pay account.

15. Every deserter shall forfeit all pay and allowances due at the time of desertion. Stoppages and fines shall be paid from his future earnings, if he is apprehended and continued in service; otherwise, from his arrears of pay.

16. No deserter shall receive pay before trial, or till restored to duty without trial by the authority competent to order the trial.

17. In case of a soldier's death, desertion, or discharge without pay, or the forfeiture of his pay by sentence of court-martial, the account due the laundress will be noted on the muster-roll.

18. When an improper payment has been made to any enlisted soldier, and disallowed in the settlement of the quartermaster's accounts, the quartermaster may report the fact to the commander of the company in which the soldier is mustered, who will note on the muster-rolls the amount to be stopped from the pay of the soldier, that it may be refunded to the quarter-

master in whose accounts the improper payment has been disallowed.

19. Authorized stoppages to reimburse the Confederate States, as for loss or damage to arms, equipments, or other public property; for extra issues of clothing; for the expense of apprehending deserters, or to reimburse individuals (as the quartermaster, laundress, &c.); forfeitures for desertion, and fines by sentence of court-martial, will be entered on the roll and paid in the order stated.

20. The quartermaster will deduct from the pay of the soldier the amount of the authorized stoppages entered on the muster-roll, descriptive list, or certificate of discharge.

21. The traveling pay is due to a discharged officer or soldier unless forfeited by sentence of a court-martial, or as provided in paragraph 23, or the discharge is by way of punishment for an offence.

22. In reckoning the traveling allowance to discharged officers or soldiers, the distance is to be estimated by the shortest mail route; if there is no mail route, by the shortest practicable route.

23. Every enlisted man discharged as a minor, or for other cause involving fraud on his part in the enlistment, or discharged by the civil authority, shall forfeit all pay and allowance due at the time of the discharge.

24. Quartermasters or other officers to whom a discharged soldier may apply, shall transmit to the quartermaster-general, with their remarks, any evidence the soldier may furnish relating to his not having received or having lost his certificate of pay due. The quartermaster-general will transmit the evidence to the Comptroller for the settlement of the account.

25. No quartermaster or other officer shall be interested in the purchase of any soldier's certificate of pay due, or other claim against the Confederate States.

26. The quartermaster-general will report to the adjutant-general any cause of neglect of company officers to furnish the proper certificates to soldiers entitled to discharge.

27. Whenever the garison is withdrawn from any post at which a chaplain is authorized to be employed, his pay and emoluments shall cease on the last day of the month next ensuing after the withdrawal of the troops. The quartermaster-general will be duly informed from the adjutant-general's office whenever the appointment and pay of the post chaplain will cease under this Regulation.

28. Funds turned over to other quartermasters, or refunded to the Treasurer, are to be entered in account current, but not in the abstracts of payments.

29. Whenever money is refunded to the Treasurer, the name of the person refunding, and the purpose for which it is done, should be stated, in order that the officers of that Department may give the proper credits.

30. When an officer of the army receives a temporary appointment from the proper authority, to a grade in the militia then in actual service in the Confederate States, higher in rank than that held by him in the army, he shall be entitled to the pay and emoluments of the grade in which he serves. But in no case can an officer receive the compensation of two military commissions or appointments at the same time.

31. Whenever the quartermaster-general shall discover that an officer has drawn pay twice for the same time, he shall report it to the adjutant-general.

32. The quartermaster-general shall transmit to the Second Auditor, in the month of May, a statement exhibiting the total amount during the year up to the 31st December preceding, of stoppages against officers and soldiers on account of ordnance and ordnance stores, that the amount may be refunded to the proper appropriations. These stoppages will be regulated by the tables of cost published by the chief of the Ordnance Department, and shall have precedence of all other claims on the pay of officers and soldiers.

33. The following returns are to be transmitted to the quartermaster-general after each payment:

1. Estimate for succeeding months (Form 1.)
2. Abstract of payments (Form 7), accompanied by the vouchers.
3. General account current, in duplicate (Form 8).
4. Monthly statement of funds, disbursements, &c., (Form 10).

34. The accounts and vouchers for the expenditures to the regular army must be kept separate and distinct from those to volunteers and militia.

35. Pay-roll of militia will be according to Form 9, the certificate at the foot to be signed by all the company officers present.

36. No militia or volunteers shall be paid till regularly mustered into service, as provided in the general regulations.

37. When volunteers are furnished with clothing, by tailors

or other persons, the furnisher may secure his pay at the first payment of the company, upon presenting to the paying quartermaster the receipt of the individual furnished, verified by the certificate of the captain as to its correctness—but this receipt will not be respected for an amount above the twenty-five dollars allowed for six months' service.

[No. 153.]

AN ACT

Concerning the transportation of soldiers and allowance for clothing of volunteers, and amendatory of the act for the establishment and organization of the army of the Confederate States.

SECTION 1. *The Congress of the Confederate States of America do enact,* When transportation cannot be furnished in kind, the discharged soldier shall be entitled to receive ten cents per mile, in lieu of all traveling pay, subsistence, forage and undrawn clothing, from the place of discharge to the place of his enlistment or enrolment, estimating the distance by the shortest mail route, and if there is no mail route, by the shortest practicable route. The foregoing to apply to all officers, non-commissioned officers, musicians, artificers, farriers, blacksmiths and privates of volunteers, when disbanded, discharged, or mustered out of service of the Confederate States; and it shall also apply to all volunteer troops as above designated, when traveling from the place of enrolment to the place of general rendezvous, or point where mustered into service: *Provided,* that nothing herein contained shall be so construed as to deprive the mounted volunteers of the allowance of forty cents a day, for the use and risk of his horse, which allowance is made from the date of his enrolment to the date of his discharge, and also for every twenty miles travel from the place of his discharge to the place of his enrolment.

SEC. 2. That the 4th section of the act of March 6th, 1861, "To provide for the public defence," be amended as follows, viz: There shall be allowed to each volunteer, to be paid to him, on the first muster and pay-rolls, after being received and mustered in the service of the Confederate States, the sum of twenty-one dollars, in lieu of clothing for six months: and thereafter the same allowance in money at every subsequent period of service for six months, in lieu of clothing: *Provided,* that the price of all clothing in kind received by said volunteers from the Confederate States Government shall be deducted first, from the money thus allowed, and if that sum be not sufficient, the balance shall be charged for stoppage on the muster and pay-rolls, and that all accounts arising from contracts, agreements, or arrangements for furnishing clothing to volunteers, to be duly certified by the company commanders, shall be paid out of the semi-annual allowance of money.

SEC. 3. That the 21st section of the act for the organization of the army of the Confederate States be so amended as to allow to aids-de-camp, and to adjutants, forage for the same number of horses as allowed to officers of the same grade in the mounted service.

HOWELL COBB,
President of the Congress.

Approved May 21, 1861.
JEFFERSON DAVIS.

Pay and Allowances of the Army.

GRADE.	Pay. Per month.	Forage. No. of Horses time of war.	Forage. No. of Horses time of peace.
Brigadier-General,	$301 00	4	3
Aid to Brigadier-General in addition to pay of Lieutenant,	35 00		
Colonel of Engineers, Artillery, Cavalry, and of the General Staff, except, the Medical Department,	210 00	3	3
Lieutenant-Colonel of Cavalry,	185 00	3	3
Major of Cavalry,	162 00	3	3
Captain of Cavalry,	140 00	3	2
First Lieutenant of Cavalry,	100 00	2	2
Second Lieutenant of Cavalry,	90 00	2	2
Adjutant, in addition to pay of Lieutenant,	10 00		
ARTILLERY.			
Colonel,	210 00	3	3
Lieutenant-Colonel,	185 00	3	3
Major,	150 00	3	3
Captain,	130 00		
First Lieutenant,	90 00		
Second Lieutenant,	80 00		
Adjutant, in addition to pay of Lieutenant,	10 00		

INFANTRY.			
Colonel,	195 00	3	3
Lieutenant-Colonel,	170 00	3	3
Major,	150 00	3	3
Captain,	130 00		
First Lieutenant,	90 00		
Second Lieutenant,	80 00		
Adjutant, in addition to pay as Lieutenant,	10 00		
MEDICAL STAFF.			
Surgeon-General, $3,000 per annum.			
Surgeon of ten years' service,	200 00	3	3
Surgeon of less than ten years' service,	162 00	3	3
Assistant Surgeon of ten year's service,	150 00	2	2
Assistant Surgeon of five years' service,	130 00	2	2
Assistant Surgeon of less than five years' service,	110 00	2	2
ENLISTED MEN.			
Sergeant or Master Workmen of Engineers, Master Armorer, Master Carriage Maker, and Master Blacksmith, each,	34 00		
Corporal or Overseer of Engineers, Armorer, Carriage Maker and Blacksmith of Ordnance, each	20 00		
Private—First Class, or Artificer of Engineers and Ordnance,	17 00		
Private—Second Class, or Laborer and Musician of Engineers, and Laborer of Ordnance,	13 00		
Sergeant-Major of Cavalry and Infantry,	21 00		
Quartermaster-Sergeant of Cavalry and Infantry,	21 00		
Principal Musicians',	21 00		
Chief Bugler,	21 00		
First Sergeant of Cavalry and Infantry,	20 00		
Sergeant of Cavalry and Infantry,	17 00		
Corporal of Cavalry, Artillery, Infantry, Artificers, Farriers and Blacksmiths,	13 00		
Musician of Cavalry.	13 00		
Musician of Artillery and Infantry,	12 00		
Private—Cavalry.	12 00		

Pay and Allowances of the Army.—Continued.

Private—Artillery and Infantry,	11 00		
Ordnance Sergeant,	21 00		
Hospital Steward appointed by the Secretary of War and Hospital Steward at posts of more than four companies,	21 00		
Hospital Steward,	20 00		
Hospital Matron,	6 00		
Chaplain.	50 00		

NOTE.—Brigadier-General commanding in chief a separate Army actually in the field, $100 per month additional.

Lieutenants serving with the company of Sappers and Miners, and officers of Artillery serving in Light Artillery or on Ordnance duty, receive Cavalry pay.

In addition to pay, as above stated (excepting Surgeon-General) $9 per month is allowed for every five years' service in the Army of the United States and Confederate States.

Subalterns of the line detailed by the War Department as Assistant Quartermasters or as Assistant Commissaries of Subsistence, receive in addition to pay in the line, $20 per month, while engaged in the duties of those Departments; but although the officer may be serving in both, he can draw this allowance for one Department only.

Tables of the Daily Pay of the Army.

DAYS.	$5 per month.	$6 per month.	$6⅔ per month.	$7 per month.	$7⅓ per month.	$8 per month.	$9 per month.	$10 per month.	$11 per month.	$12 per month.	$13 per month.	$16 per month.	$20 per month.	$23 per month.	$25 per month.	$26⅔ per month.	$30 per month.	$33⅓ per month.	$40 per month.	$50 per month.	$60 per month.	75 per month.
I,	16	20	22	23	24	26	30	33	36	40	43	53	66	76	83	88	1 00	1 11	1 33	1 66	2 00	2 50
II,	33	40	44	46	48	53	60	66	73	80	86	1 06	1 33	1 53	1 69	1 77	2 00	2 22	2 66	3 33	4 00	5 00
III,	50	60	66	70	73	80	90	1 00	1 10	1 20	1 30	1 60	2 00	2 30	2 50	2 66	3 00	3 33	4 00	5 00	6 00	7 50
IV,	66	80	88	93	97	1 06	1 20	1 33	1 46	1 60	1 73	2 13	2 66	3 06	3 33	3 55	4 00	4 44	5 33	6 66	8 00	10 00
V,	83	1 00	1 11	1 16	1 22	1 33	1 50	1 66	1 83	2 00	2 16	2 66	3 33	3 83	4 16	4 44	5 00	5 55	6 66	8 33	10 00	12 50
VI,	1 00	1 20	1 33	1 40	1 46	1 60	1 80	2 00	2 20	2 40	2 60	3 20	4 00	4 60	5 00	5 33	6 00	6 66	8 00	10 00	12 00	15 00
VII,	1 16	1 40	1 55	1 63	1 71	1 86	1 10	2 33	2 56	2 80	3 03	3 73	4 66	5 36	5 83	6 22	7 00	7 77	9 33	11 66	14 00	17 50
VIII,	1 33	1 60	1 07	1 86	1 75	2 13	2 40	2 66	2 93	3 20	3 46	4 26	5 33	6 13	6 66	7 10	8 00	8 88	10 66	13 33	16 00	20 00
IX,	1 50	1 80	1 99	2 10	2 19	2 40	2 70	3 00	3 30	3 60	3 90	4 [illegible]	6 00	6 90	7 50	7 99	9 00	9 99	12 00	15 00	18 00	22 50
X,	1 66	2 00	2 22	2 33	2 44	2 66	3 00	3 33	3 66	4 00	4 33	5 33	6 66	7 66	8 33	8 88	10 00	11 11	13 33	16 66	20 00	25 00
XI,	1 83	1 20	2 44	2 56	2 68	2 83	3 30	3 66	4 03	4 40	4 76	5 86	7 33	8 43	9 16	9 77	11 00	12 22	14 66	18 3[illegible]	22 00	27 50
XII,	2 00	[illegible] 40	2 66	[illegible] 60	2 93	3 20	3 60	4 00	4 [illegible]	4 80	5 20	6 40	8 00	9 20	10 00	10 66	12 00	13 33	16 00	20 00	24 00	30 00
XIII,	2 16	2 60	3 98	3 [illegible]	3 17	3 46	3 90	4 33	4 [illegible]	5 20	5 63	6 93	8 66	9 96	10 83	11 55	13 00	14 44	17 33	21 66	26 00	32 50
XIV,	2 33	2 80	3 10	3 [illegible]	3 42	3 73	4 20	4 66	5 13	5 60	6 06	7 46	9 33	10 73	11 66	12 44	14 00	15 56	18 66	23 33	28 06	35 00
XV,	2 50	3 00	3 33	[illegible]	[illegible] 66	4 00	4 50	5 00	5 50	6 00	6 50	8 00	10 00	11 50	12 50	13 33	15 00	16 66	20 00	25 00	[illegible]	37 50
XVI,	2 66	3 20	3 55	[illegible]	[illegible] 90	4 26	4 80	[illegible] 33	5 86	6 40	6 93	8 53	10 66	12 26	13 33	14 21	16 00	17 77	21 33	26 66	[illegible] 00	40 00
XVII,	2 83	3 40	3 77	[illegible]	[illegible]	4 53	5 10	5 66	6 23	6 80	7 36	9 06	11 33	13 03	14 16	15 10	17 00	18 88	22 66	28 33	34 00	42 50
XVIII,	3 00	3 60	3 [illegible]	4 20	[illegible]	4 80	5 40	6 00	6 60	7 20	7 50	9 60	12 00	13 80	15 00	15 99	18 00	19 99	24 00	30 00	36 00	45 00
XIX,	3 16	3 80	4 21	4 43	4 64	5 06	5 70	6 33	6 96	7 60	8 23	10 13	12 66	14 56	15 83	16 88	19 00	21 11	25 33	31 66	38 00	47 50
XX,	3 33	4 00	4 44	4 66	4 88	5 33	6 00	6 66	7 33	8 00	8 66	10 66	13 33	15 33	16 66	17 77	20 00	22 22	26 66	33 33	40 00	50 00
XXI,	3 50	4 20	4 66	4 90	5 13	5 60	6 30	7 00	7 70	8 40	9 10	11 20	14 00	16 10	17 50	18 66	21 00	23 33	28 00	35 00	42 00	52 50
XXII,	3 66	4 40	4 81	5 13	5 37	5 86	6 60	7 33	8 06	8 80	9 53	11 73	14 66	16 86	18 23	19 55	22 00	24 44	29 33	36 66	44 00	55 00
XXIII,	3 83	4 60	5 10	5 26	5 61	6 13	6 90	7 66	8 43	9 20	9 96	12 26	15 23	17 63	19 16	20 43	23 00	25 55	30 66	38 33	46 00	57 50
XXIV,	4 00	4 80	5 22	5 60	5 86	6 40	7 20	8 00	8 80	9 60	10 40	12 80	16 00	18 40	20 00	21 32	24 00	26 66	32 00	40 00	48 00	60 00
XXV,	4 16	5 00	5 55	5 83	6 10	6 66	7 50	8 33	9 16	10 00	10 83	13 33	16 66	19 16	20 83	22 21	25 00	27 77	33 33	41 66	50 00	62 50
XXVI,	4 33	5 20	5 7[illegible]	6 06	6 35	6 93	7 80	8 66	9 63	10 40	11 26	13 86	17 33	19 93	21 66	23 10	26 00	28 88	34 66	43 33	52 00	65 00
XXVII,	4 50	5 40	5 99	6 30	6 59	7 20	8 10	9 00	9 90	10 80	11 20	14 40	18 00	20 70	22 50	23 99	27 00	29 99	36 00	45 00	54 00	67 50
XXVIII,	4 66	5 60	6 21	6 53	6 81	7 46	8 40	9 33	10 26	11 20	12 13	14 93	18 66	21 46	23 33	24 88	28 00	33 11	37 33	46 66	56 00	70 00
XXIX,	4 83	5 80	6 43	6 76	7 08	7 73	8 70	9 66	10 63	11 60	12 56	15 46	19 33	22 23	24 16	25 77	29 00	32 22	38 66	48 33	58 00	72 50
XXX,	5 00	6 00	6 66	7 00	7 33	8 00	9 00	10 00	11 00	12 00	14 00	16 00	20 00	23 00	25 00	26 66	30 00	33 33	40 00	50 00	60 00	75 00

Form No. 1.

Estimate of Funds required for the Pay, Forage, and Clothing of the —— Regiment of ——, stationed at ——, for —— months, founded on the actual number of said troops.

Enumeration of Troops.	Period.		Pay.		Forage.		Amount.	
	From.	To.	$.	Cents.	$.	Cents.	$.	Cents.
— Colonel, . @ $ per month,								
— Lieut. Colonel, . @ $ "								
— Majors, . @ $ "								
— Surgeon. . @ $ "								
— Ass't Surgeon, . @ $ "								
— Captains, @ $ "								
— 1st Lieutenants, @ $ "								
— 2d Lieutenants, @ $ "								
— Sergeant-major, @ $ "								
— Qr. Mr. Sergeant, @ $ "								
— 1st Sergeants, . @ $ "								
— Sergeants, . @ $ "								
— Corporals, . @ $ "								
— Musicians, . @ $ "								
— Farriers and Black-smiths, . @ $ "								
— Privates, . @ $ "								
— Add six months clothing allowance, for —— men, . . .								
	Total amount, ...							
	Deduct balance on hand, ...							
	Amount required, ... $							

Examined and approved.

Commanding

—— ——, *Ass't Quartermaster.*
—— *Regiment of* ——.

Form No. 2.

Consolidated Estimate of Funds required for the Pay, Forage and Clothing of the following Troops for —— months, commencing the —— of —— 1861, and ending the —— of —— 1861.

Regiment or corps	Generals.	Aids-de-Camps.	Colonels.	Lieutenant-Colonels.	Majors.	Surgeons.	Assistant Surgeons.	Captains.	1st Lieutenants.	2d Lieutenants.	Chaplains.	Sergeant-Majors.	Quartermaster Sergeants.	1st Sergeants.	Sergeants.	Corporals.	Musicians.	Farriers and Blacksmiths.	Privates.	PAY.		FORAGE.		CLOTHING.		AMOUNT.	
																				Dolls.	Cents.	Dolls.	Cents.	Dolls.	Cents.	Dols	Cts.
Field and staff,																											
— Regiment of —																											
— Regiment of —																											
— Regiment of —																											

Total amount required, ... $

Station ——.

Date ——.

—— ——, *Chief A. Q. Master.*

Approved: —— ——, *Commanding.*

FORM No. 3.

Receipts to be rendered by Quartermasters for Remittances.

Received of ——, this —— day of —— 18 , at ——, in the State of ——, on ——, dated the —— day of —— 18 , the sum of —— dollars and —— cents, on account of the pay, &c. of the Army of the Confederate States, as follows:

Pay, ...	$
Forage, ...	
Clothing, ...	
Amount, . .	$

For which sum I am accountable.

(Signed duplicates.)

FORM No. 4.—OFFICERS' PAY ACCOUNT.

The Confederate States, to ——— ———, DR.

On what account.	Commencement and expiration.		Term of service charged.		Pay per month.		Amount.		Remarks.
	From.	To.	Months.	Days.	Dolls.	Cts.	Dolls.	Cts.	
PAY—									
For myself, . .									
For myself for —— years' service, .									
FORAGE—									
For horse, .									

I hereby certify that the foregoing account is accurate and just: that I have not been absent without leave during any part of the time charged for; that I have not received pay, forage, or received money in lieu of any part thereof, for any part of the time therein charged; that the horses were actually kept in service and were mustered for the whole time charged; that for the whole of the time charged for my staff appointment, I actually and legally held the appointment and did duty in the department; that I have been a commissioned officer for the number of years stated in the charge for every additional five years' service; that I am not in arrears with the Confederate States, on any account whatsoever; and that the last payment I received was from ———, and to the ——— day of ——— 18 .

I at the same time acknowledge that I have received of ——— ———, this ——— day of ——— 18 , the sum of ——— dollars, being the amount in full of said account.

Pay . .
To —— years' service,
Forage, . :

Amount. .

(*Signed duplicates.*)

FORM No. 5.

Certificate to be given a soldier at the time of his discharge.

I certify that the within named ——— a ——— of Captain ——— company (——.) of the ——— regiment of ———, born in ———, in the State of ———, aged ——— years, ——— feet, ——— inches high, ——— complexion, ——— eyes, ——— hair, and by ——— a ——— was enlisted by ——— at ——— on the ——— day of ——— 186 , to serve ——— years, and is now entitled to discharge by reason of ———

The said ——— was last paid by ———, to include the ——— day of ——— 186 , and has pay due from that time to the present date.

There is due to him ——— dollars traveling expenses from ———, the place of discharge to ———, the place of enrolment, transportation not being furnished in kind.

There is due him ———.

He is indebted to the Confederate States ——— dollars, on account of ———.

Given in duplicate at ———, this ——— day of ——— 186 .

——— ———

Commanding Company.

NOTE.—When this certificate is transferred it must be on the back, witnessed by a commissioned officer, if practicable, or by some other reputable person well known to the Quartermaster.

FORM No. 6.

Account to be made by Quartermaster.

For pay from —— of ——, 186 , to —— of ——, 186 , being —— months, and —— days, at —— dollars per month, .		
For pay for traveling from ——— to ———, being —— miles, at ———, ...		
Amount, ...		
Deduct for clothing overdrawn, ...		
Balance paid, ...		

Received of ———, C. S. Army, this —— day of ———, 186 , ——— dollars and ——— cents, in full of the above account.

(Signed duplicates.)

Witness: ——— ———.

FORM No. 7.

Abstract of payments made by ——, *Quartermaster, for the* —— *months of* ——.

No. of voucher.	Date of payment.	To whom paid.	Rank or grade.	Corps.	Commencement and expiration.		Pay.		Forage.						Amount.		Remarks.
					From.	To.	Dols.	Cts.	Dols.	Cts.	Dols.	Cts.	Dols.	Cts.	Dols.	Cts.	

I do hereby certify that the foregoing Abstract contains an accurate statement of the payments made by me, as therein expressed.

—— ——, *Quartermaster*.

Form No. 8.—Account Current.

Dr. *The Confederate States, in account current with* , *Quartermaster Confederate States Army.* Cr.

Date.		Pay.		Subsistence.		Forage.		Amount.		Date.		Pay.		Subsistence.		Forage.		Amount.	
		Dolls.	Cents.	Dolls.	Cents.	Dolls.	Cents.	Dolls.	Cents.			Dolls.	Cents.	Dolls.	Cents.	Dolls.	Cents.	Dolls.	Cents.
18	For amount expended, as per abstract and vouchers herewith, in paying the troops since the — of —— 18—, the date of the last account rendered, .										By balance to be accounted for, as stated in last account, . . .								
	For amount turned over to ——. .									18	By cash received of ——, as per my receipt dated the — day of —— 18—, .								
	Due the Confederate States, to be accounted for in the next account, .									18	By amount received of ——, for ——, .								
	Amount, .										Amount. .								
											By balance brought down. . .								

I certify that the above is a true account of all public money received by me, not heretofore accounted for, and that the disbursements have been fully made.

Stated at ——, this —— day of —— 18

(Duplicate.)

——, *Quartermaster.*

Form No. 9.

We, the subscribers, do hereby acknowledge to have received of   , Quartermaster, the sums annexed to our names respectively, being the full of our pay and allowances for the period herein expressed, having signed duplicates thereof.

8

No.	Name.	Period of service.				Pay per month.	Amount of pay.	Forage.	40 cents per day, use of horses, arms, &c.	Traveling allowance.		Total amount.	Stoppages.	Balances paid.	Signature.	Witness.	Remarks.
		Commencement.	Expiration.	Months.	Days.												

We certify, on honor, that we actually owned and kept in service the horses for which we have received payment, for the whole of the time charged. We also certify that the non commissioned officers and privates of the company to which we belong, who are made up for pay, &c., as having horses and arms, actually owned and had them in service for the time paid for, although, in some cases, they may not have been valued. We also certify that we witnessed the payment of the whole company.

——— ———, *Captain.*

——— ———, *1st Lieut.*

——— ———, *2d Lieut.*

——— ———, *Ensign.*

Form No. 10.

Statement of moneys received and expended, and on hand, for the month ending ——————.

Date.			Pay.	Forage.	Effects of deceased soldiers.	Overdrawn clothing.	Ordnance.	Equipments.	Quartermaster's stores.	Militia.	Amount.	Remarks.
	Amount on hand from last month,											
	Received from the treasurer,											
	Received from Quartermaster,											
	Received from ——,											
	Total received,	$										
	Expended in paying the troops,											
	Turned over to Quartermaster,											
	Total expended,	$										
	Balance to be accounted for,	$										

Accountable for ——— iron safe.

—— ———, *Quartermaster.*

WORKING PARTIES.

When it is necessary to employ the army at work on fortifications, in surveys, in cutting roads, and other constant labor of not less than ten days, the non-commissioned officers and soldiers so employed are enrolled as extra-duty men, and are allowed twenty-five cents a day when employed as laborers and teamsters, and forty cents a day when employed as mechanics, at all stations east of the Rocky Mountains, and thirty-five and fifty cents per day, respectively, at all stations west of those mountains.

Enlisted men of the Ordnance and Engineer Departments, and artificers of artillery, are not entitled to this allowance when employed in their appropriate work.

Soldiers shall not be employed as extra-duty men for any labor in camp or garrison which can properly be performed by fatigue parties.

No extra-duty men, except those required for the ordinary service of the Quartermaster, Commissary, and Medical Departments, and sadlers in mounted companies, will be employed without previous authority from department head-quarters, except in case of necessity, which shall be promptly reported to the department commander.

Extra-duty pay of the soldier in a mounted company will be charged on the company muster-roll, to be paid by the Quartermaster and refunded by the Ordnance Department. Extra-duty pay of cooks and nurses in the hospital service will be paid by the Quartermaster, in the absence of a medical disbursing officer, and refunded by the Medical Department.

The officer commanding a working party will conform to the directions and plans of the engineer or other officer directing the work, without regard to rank.

A day's work shall not exceed ten hours in summer, nor eight in winter. Soldiers are paid in proportion for any greater number of hours they are employed each day. Summer is considered to commence on the 1st of April, and winter on the 1st of October.

Although the necessities of the service may require soldiers to be ordered on working parties as a duty, commanding officers are to bear in mind that fitness for military service by instruction and discipline is the object for which the army is kept on foot, and that they are not to employ the troops when not in the field, and especially the mounted troops, in labors that interfere with their military duties and exercises, except in case of immediate necessity, which shall be forthwith reported for the orders of the War Department.

PUBLIC PROPERTY, MONEY, AND ACCOUNTS.

All officers of the Pay, Commissary, and Quartermaster's Departments, and military store-keepers, shall, previous to their entering on the duties of their respective offices, give good and sufficient bonds to the Confederate States fully to account for all moneys and public property which they may receive, in such sums as the Secretary of War shall direct; and the officers aforesaid shall renew their bonds every four years, and oftener if the Secretary of War shall so require, and whenever they receive a new commission or appointment.

The sureties to the bond shall be bound jointly and severally for the whole amount of the bond, and shall satisfy the Secretary of War that they are worth jointly double the amount of the bond, by the affidavit of each surety, stating that he is worth, over and above his debts and liabilities, the amount of the bond or such other sum as he may specify, and each surety shall state his place of residence.

The chiefs of disbursing departments who submit requisitions for money to be remitted to disbursing officers, shall take care that no more money than actually needed is in the hands of any officer.

The Treasury Department having provided, by arrangement with the assistant treasurers at various points, secure depositories for funds in the hands of disbursing officers, all disbursing officers are required to avail themselves, as far as possible, of this arrangement, by depositing with the assistant treasurer such funds as are not wanted for immediate use, and drawing the same in convenient sums as wanted.

No public funds shall be exchanged except for gold and silver. When the funds furnished are gold and silver, all payments shall be in gold and silver. When the funds furnished are drafts, they shall be presented at the place of payment, and paid according to law; and payments shall be made in the funds so received for the drafts, unless said funds or said drafts can be exchanged for gold and silver at par. If any disbursing officer shall violate any of these provisions, he shall be suspended by the Secretary of War, and reported to the President, and promptly removed from office or restored to his trust and duties as to the President may seem just and proper.

No disbursing officer shall accept, or receive, or transmit to the Treasury to be allowed in his favor, any receipt or voucher from a creditor of the Confederate States without having paid to such creditor, in such funds as he received for disbursement, or such other funds as he is authorized by the preceding article to take in exchange, the full amount specified in such receipt or voucher; and every such act shall be deemed to be a conversion to his own use of the amount specified in such receipt or voucher. And no officer in the military service charged with the safe keeping, transfer, or disbursement of public money, shall convert to his own use, or invest in any kind of merchandize or property, or loan with or without interest, or deposit in any bank, or exchange for any funds, except as allowed in the preceding article, any public money intrusted to him; any every such act shall be deemed to be a felony and an embezzlement of so much money as may be so taken, converted, invested, used, loaned, deposited, or exchanged.

Any officer who shall directly or indirectly sell or dispose of, for a premium, any treasury note, draft, warrant, or other public security in his hands for disbursement, or sell or dispose of the proceeds or avails thereof without making returns of such premium and accounting therefor by charging it in his accounts to the credit of the Confederate States, will forthwith be dismissed by the President.

If any disbursing officer shall bet at cards or any game of hazard, his commanding officer shall suspend his functions and require him to turn over all the public funds in his keeping, and shall immediately report the case to the proper bureau of the War Department.

All officers are forbid to give or take any receipt in blank for public money or property; but in all cases the voucher shall be made out in full, and the true date, place, and exact amount of money, in words, shall be written out in the receipt before it is signed.

When a signature is not written by the hand of the party, it must be witnessed.

No advance of public money shall be made, except advances to disbursing officers, and advances by order of the War Department to officers on distant stations, where they cannot receive their pay and emoluments regularly; but in all cases of contracts for the performance of any service, or the delivery of articles of any description, payment shall not exceed the value of the service rendered, or of the articles delivered, previously to such payment.

No officer disbursing or directing the disbursement of money for the military service shall be concerned, directly or indirectly, in the purchase or sale, for commercial purposes, of any article intended for, making a part of, or appertaining to the department of the public service in which he is engaged, nor shall take or apply to his own use any gain or emolument for negotiating or transacting any public business other than what is or may be allowed by law.

No wagon-master or forage-master shall be interested or concerned, directly or indirectly, in any wagon or other means of transport employed by the Confederate States, nor in the purchase or sale of any property procured for or belonging to the Confederate States, except as the agent of the Confederate States.

No officer or agent in the military service shall purchase from any other person in the military service, or make any contract with any such person to furnish supplies or services, or make any purchase or contract in which such person shall be admitted to any share or part, or to any benefit to arise therefrom.

No person in the military service whose salary, pay or emoluments is or are fixed by law or regulations, shall receive any additional pay, extra allowance, or compensation in any form whatever, for the disbursement of public money, or any other service or duty whatsoever, unless the same shall be authorized by law, and explicitly set out in the appropriation.

All accounts of expenditures shall set out a sufficient explanation of the object, necessity, and propriety of the expenditure.

The facts on which an account depends must be stated and vouched by the certificate of an officer, or other sufficient evidence.

If any account paid on the certificate of an officer to the facts is afterwards disallowed for error of fact in the certificate, it shall pass to the credit of the disbursing officer, and be charged to the officer who gave the certificate.

An officer shall have credit for an expenditure of money or property made in obedience to the order of his commanding officer. If the expenditure is disallowed, it shall be charged to the officer who ordered it.

Disbursing officers, when they have the money, shall pay cash, and not open an account. Heads of bureaus shall take care, by timely remittances, to obviate the necessity of any purchase on credit.

When a disbursing officer is relieved, he shall certify the outstanding debts to his successor, and transmit an account of the same to the head of the bureau, and turn over his public money and property appertaining to the service from which he is relieved, to his successor, unless otherwise ordered.

This chief of each military bureau of the War Department shall, under the direction of the Secretary of War, regulate, as far as practicable, the employment of hired persons required for the administrative service of his department.

When practicable, persons hired in the military service shall be paid at the end of the calendar month, and when discharged. Separate pay-rolls shall be made for each month.

When a hired person is discharged and not paid, a certified statement of his account shall be given him.

Property, paid for or not, must be taken up on the return, and accounted for when received.

No officer has authority to insure public property or money.

Disbursing officers are not authorized to settle with heirs, executors, or administrators, except by instructions from the proper bureau of the War Department upon accounts duly audited and certified by the proper accounting officers of the Treasury.

Public horses, mules, oxen, tools, and implements shall be branded conspicuously C. S. before being used in service, and all other public property that it may be useful to mark; and all public property having the brand of the C. S. when sold or condemned, shall be branded with the letter C.

No public property shall be used, nor labor hired for the public be employed, for any private use whatsoever not authorized by the regulations of the service.

When public property becomes damaged, except by fair wear and tear, the officer accountable for the property shall report the case to the commanding officer, who shall appoint a board of survey of two or more officers to examine the property and ascertain the cause and amount of damage, and whether by any fault of any person in the military service, and report the facts and their opinion to him; which report, with his opinion thereon, he shall transmit to the chief of the department to which the property appertains, and give a copy to the officer accountable for the property and to the person chargeable for the damage.

If any article of public property be lost or damaged by neglect or fault of any officer or soldier, he shall pay the value of such article, or amount of damage, or cost of repairs, and be proceeded against as the Articles of War provide, if he demand a trial by court-martial, or the circumstances require it.

Charges against a soldier shall be set against his pay on the muster-roll. Charges against an officer to be set against his pay shall be promptly reported to the Secretary of War.

If any article of public property be embezzled, or by neglect lost or damaged by any person hired in the public service, the value or damage shall be charged to him, and set against any pay or money due him.

Public property lost or destroyed in the military service must be accounted for by affidavit, or the certificate of a commissioned officer, or other satisfactory evidence.

Affidavits or depositions may be taken before any officer in the list, as follows, when recourse cannot be had to any before-named on said list, which fact shall be certified by the officer offering the evidence: 1st. a civil magistrate competent to administer oaths; 2d. a judge advocate; 3d. the recorder of a garrison or regimental court-martial; 4th. the Adjutant of a regiment; 5th. a commissioned officer.

When military stores or other army supplies are unsuitable to the service, the officer in charge thereof shall report the case to the commanding officer, who shall refer the report, with his opinion thereon, to the bureau of the department to which the property appertains, for the order in the case of the Secretary of War. But if, from the nature or condition of the property or exigency of the service, it be necessary to act without the delay of such reference, in such case of necessity the commanding officer shall appoint a board of survey, composed of two or more competent officers, to examine the property and report to him, subject to his approval, what disposition the public interest requires to be made of it; which he shall cause to be made, and report the case to the proper bureau of the War Department for the information of the Secretary of War. These cases of necessity arise when the property is of perishable nature and cannot be kept, or when the expense of keeping it is too great in proportion to its value, or when the troops, in movement, would be compelled to abandon it. Horses incurably unfit for any public service may also constitute a case of necessity, but shall be put to death only in case of an incurable wound or contagious disorder.

When military stores or other army supplies are reported to the War Department as unsuitable to the service, a proper inspection or survey of them shall be made by an Inspector-General, or such suitable officer or officers as the Secretary of War may appoint for that purpose. Separate inventories of the stores, according to the disposition to be made of them, shall accompany the inspection report: as of articles to be repaired, to be broken up, to be sold, of no use or value, and to be dropped, &c., &c. The inspection report and inventories shall show the exact condition of the different articles.

Military stores and other army supplies found unsuitable to the public service, after inspection by an Inspector-General, and ordered for sale, shall be sold for cash at auction, on due public notice, and in such market as the public interest may require. The officer making the sale will bid in and suspend the sale when, in his opinion, better prices may be got. Expenses of the sale will be paid from the proceeds. The auctioneer's verified account of the sale in detail, and the vouchers for the expenses of the sale, will be reported to the chief of the department to which the property belonged. The net proceeds will be applied as the Secretary of War may direct.

No officer making returns of property shall drop from his return any public property as worn out or unserviceable until it has been condemned, after proper inspection, and ordered to be so dropped.

An officer issuing stores shall deliver or transmit to the receiving officer an exact list of them in duplicate invoices, and the receiving officer shall return him duplicate receipts.

When an officer to whom stores are forwarded has reason to suppose them miscarried, he shall promptly inform the issuing and forwarding officer, and the bureau of the department to which the property appertains.

When stores received do not correspond in amount or quality with the invoice, they will be examined by a board of survey, and their report communicated to the proper bureau, to the issuing and forwarding officer, and to the officer authorized to pay the transportation account. Damages recovered from the carrier or other party liable, will be refunded to the proper department.

On the death of any officer in charge of public property or money, the commanding officer shall appoint a board of survey to take an inventory of the same, which he shall forward to the proper bureau of the War Department, and he shall designate an officer to take charge of the said property or money till orders in the case are received from the proper authority.

When an officer in charge of public property is removed from the care of it, the commanding officer shall designate an officer to receive it, or take charge of it himself, till a successor be regularly appointed. Where no officer can remain to receive it, the commanding officer will take suitable means to secure it, and report the facts to the proper authority.

Every officer having public money to account for, and failing to render his account thereof quarter-yearly, with the vouchers necessary to its correct and prompt settlement, within three months after the expiration of the quarter if resident in the Confederate States, and within six months if resident in a foreign country, will be promptly dismissed by the President, unless he shall explain the default to the satisfaction of the President.

Every officer intrusted with public money or property shall render all prescribed returns and accounts to the bureau of the department in which he is serving, where all such returns and accounts shall pass through a rigid administrative scrutiny before the money accounts are transmitted to the proper offices of the Treasury Department for settlement.

The head of the bureau shall cause his decision on each account to be endorsed on it. He shall bring to the notice of the Secretary of War all accounts and matters of account that require or merit it. When an account is suspended or disallowed, the bureau shall notify it to the officer, that he may have early opportunity to submit explanations or take an appeal to the Secretary of War.

When an account is suspended or disallowed in the proper office of the Treasury Department, or explanation or evidence required from the officer, it shall be promptly notified to him by the head of the military bureau. And all vouchers, evidence, or explanation returned by him to the Treasury Department shall pass through the bureau.

Chiefs of the disbursing departments shall, under the direction of the Secretary of War, designate, as far as practicable, the places where the principal contracts and purchases shall be made and supplies procured for distribution.

All purchases and contracts for supplies or services for the army, except personal services, when the public exigencies do not require the immediate delivery of the articles or performance of the service, shall be made by advertising a sufficient time previously for proposals respecting the same.

The officer advertising for proposals shall, when the intended purchase or contract is considerable, transmit forthwith a copy of the advertisement and report of the case to the proper bureau of the War Department.

Contracts will be made with the lowest responsible bidder, and purchases from the lowest bidder who produces the proper article. But when such lowest bids are unreasonable, they will be rejected, and bids again invited by public notice; and all bids and advertisements shall be sent to the bureau.

When sealed bids are required, the time of opening them shall be specified, and bidders have privilege to be present at the opening.

When immediate delivery or performance is required by the public exigency, the articles or service required may be procured by open purchase or contract at the places, and in the mode in which such articles are usually bought and sold, or such services engaged, between individuals.

Contracts shall be made in quadruplicate; one to be kept by the officer, one by the contractor, and two to be sent to the military bureau, one of which for the office of the Second Comptroller of the Treasury.

The contractor shall give bond, with good and sufficient security, for the true and faithful performance of his contract, and each surety shall state his place of residence.

An express condition shall be inserted in contracts that no member of congress shall be admitted to any share or part therein, or any benefit to arise therefrom.

No contract shall be made except under a law authorizing it, or an appropriation adequate to its fulfillment, except contracts by the Secretary of War for the subsistence or clothing of the army, or the Quartermaster's Department.

It is the duty of every commanding officer to enforce a rigid economy in the public expenses.

All estimates for supplies of property or money for the public service within a department shall be forwarded through the commander of the department, and carefully revised by him. And all such estimates shall go through the immediate commander, if such there be, of the officer rendering the estimate, as of the post or regiment, who shall be required by the department commander to revise the estimates for the service of his own command.

The administrative control exercised by department commanders shall, when troops are in the field, devolve on commanders of divisions; or, when the command is less than a division, on the commander of the whole.

No land shall be purchased for the Confederate States except under a law authorizing such purchase.

No public money shall, be expended for the purchase of any land, nor for erecting armories, arsenals, forts, fortifications, or other permanent public buildings, until the written opinion of the Attorney General shall be had in favor of the validity of the title to the land or site, nor, if the land be within any State of the Confederate States, until a cession of the jurisdiction by the Legislature of the State.

No permanent buildings for the army, as barracks, quarters, hospitals, store-houses, offices, or stables, or piers, or wharves, shall be erected but by order of the Secretary of War, and according to the plan directed by him, and in consequence of appropriations made by law. And no alteration shall be made in any such public building without authority from the War Department.

Complete title papers, with full and exact maps, plans, and drawings of the public lands purchased, appropriated, or designed for permanent military fortifications, will be collected, recorded, and filed in the Bureau of the Corps of Engineers; of the public lands appropriated or designated for armories, arsenals, and ordnance depots, will be collected, recorded, and filed in the Ordnance Bureau; of all other land belonging to the Confederate States, and under the charge of the War Department for barracks, posts, cantonments, or other military uses, will be collected, recorded, and filed in the office of the Quartermaster General of the army.

A copy of the survey of the land at each post, fort, arsenal, and depot, furnished from the proper bureau, will be carefully preserved in the office of the commanding officer.

TROOPS ON BOARD OF TRANSPORTS.

Military commanders charged with the embarkation of troops, and officers of the Quartermaster's Department intrusted with the selection of the transports, will take care that the vessels are entirely seaworthy and proper for such service, and that suitable arrangements are made in them for the health and comfort of the troops.

If, in the opinion of the officer commanding the troops to be embarked, the vessel is not proper or suitably arranged, the officer charged with the embarkation shall cause her to be inspected by competent and experienced persons.

Immediately after embarking, the men will be assigned to quarters, equal parties on each side of the ship, and no man will be allowed to loiter or sleep on the opposite side. As far as practicable, the men of each company will be assigned to the same part of the vessel, and the squads, in the same manner, to contiguous berths.

Arms will be placed, if there be no racks, as to be secure from injury, and enable the men to handle them promptly—bayonets unfixed and in scabbard.

Ammunition in cartridge-boxes to be so placed as to be entirely secure from fire; reserve ammunition to be reported to the master of the transport, with request that he designate a safe place of deposit. Frequent inspections will be made of the service ammunition, to insure its safety and good condition.

No officer is to sleep out of his ship, or to quit his ship, without the sanction of the officer commanding on board.

The guard will be proportioned to the number of sentinels required. At sea the guard will mount with side arms only. The officer of the guard will be officer of the day.

Sentinels will be kept over the fires, with buckets of water at hand, promptly to extinguish fires. Smoking is prohibited *between decks or in the cabins*, at all times; nor shall any lights be allowed between decks, except such ship lanterns as the master of the transport may direct, or those carried by the officer of the day in the execution of his duty.

Regulations will be adopted to enable companies or messes to cook in turn; no others than those whose turn it is, will be allowed to loiter around or approach the galleys or other cooking places.

The commanding officer will make arrangements, in concert with the master of the vessel, for calling the troops to quarters, so that in case of alarm, by storm, or fire, or the approach of the enemy, every man may repair promptly to his station. But he will take care not to crowd the deck. The troops not wanted at the guns or to assist the sailors, and those who cannot be advantageously employed with small arms, will be formed as a reserve between decks.

All the troops will turn out at A. M., without arms or uniform, and (in warm weather) without shoes or stockings; when every individual will be clean, his hands, face and feet washed, and his hair combed. The same personal inspection will be repeated thirty minutes before sunset. The cooks alone may be exempt from *one* of these inspections per day, if necessary.

Recruits or awkward men will be exercised in the morning and evening in the use of arms, an hour each time, when the weather will permit.

Officers will enforce cleanliness as indispensable to health. When the weather will permit, bedding will be brought on deck every morning for airing. Tubs may be fixed on the forecastle for bathing, or the men may be placed in the *chains* and have buckets of water thrown over them.

Between decks will not be washed oftener than once a week, and only when the weather is fine. The boards of the lower berths will be removed once or twice a week to change the straw. Under the direction of the Surgeon and the officer of the day, frequent fumigations will be performed between decks. The materials required are—common salt, four ounces; powdered oxide of manganese, one ounce; sulphuric acid one ounce, diluted with two ounces of water. The diluted acid is poured over the other ingredients in a basin placed in a hot sand-bath. Solutions of chloride of lime and chloride of zinc are excellent disinfecting agents.

During voyages in hot weather, the master of the vessel will be desired to provide wind-sails, which will be kept constantly hung up, and frequently examined, to see that they draw well and are not obstructed.

During cooking hours, the officers of companies visit the camboose, and see that the messes are well prepared. The coppers and other cooking utensils are to be regularly and well washed both *before* and *after* use.

The bedding will be replaced in the berths at sunset, or at an earlier hour when there is a prospect of bad weather; and at *tattoo* every man not on duty will be in his berth. To insure the execution of this regulation, the officer of the day, with a lantern, will make a tour between decks.

Lights will be extinguished at *tattoo*, except such as are placed under sentinels. The officer of the day will see to it, and report to the commanding officer. The officers' lights will be extinguished at 10 o'clock, unless special permission be given to continue them for a longer time, as in case of sickness or other emergency.

For the sake of exercise, the troops will be occasionally called to quarters by the beat *to arms*. Those appointed to the guns will be frequently exercised in the use of them. The arms and accoutrements will be frequently inspected. The metalic parts of the former will be often wiped and greased again.

The men will not be allowed to sleep on deck in hot weather or in the sun; they will be encouraged and required to take exercise on deck, in squads by succession, when necessary.

At morning and evening parades, the Surgeon will examine the men, to observe whether there be any appearance of disease.

The sick will, as far as practicable, be separated from the healthy men. On the first appearance of malignant contagion, a signal will be made for the hospital vessel (if there be one in company,) and the diseased men removed to her.

A good supply of hospital stores and medicines will be taken on each vessel, and used only for the sick and convalescent.

The Surgeon will guard the men against costiveness on approaching a hot climate. In passing through the West Indies, to the Southern coast for instance, and for some weeks after landing in those latitudes, great care is required in the use of fruit, as strangers would not be competent to judge of it, and most kinds, after long voyages, are prejudicial.

In harbor, where there is no danger from sharks, the men may bathe; but not more than ten at a time, and attended by a boat.

In fitting up a vessel for the transportation of horses, care is to be taken that the requisite arrangements are made for conveniently feeding and cleaning them, and to secure them from injury in rough weather by ropes attached to breast-straps and breeching, or by other suitable means; and especially that proper ventilation is provided by openings in the upper deck, windsails, &c. The ventilation of steamers may be assisted by using the engine for that purpose.

Horses should not be put on board after severe exercise or when heated. In hoisting them on board, the slings should be made fast to a hook at the end of the fall, or the knot tied by an expert seaman, so that it may be well secured and easily loosened. The horse should be run up quickly, to prevent him from plunging, and should be steadied by guide ropes. A halter is placed on him before he is lifted from the ground.

On board, care is to be taken that the horses are not overfed; bran should form part of their ration. The face, eyes, and nostrils of each horse are to be washed at the usual stable hours, and, occasionally, the mangers should be washed and the nostrils of the horses sponged with vinegar and water.

In loading vessels with stores for a military expedition, the cargo of each should be composed of an assortment of such stores as may be available for service in case of the non-arrival of others, and they should be placed on board in such a manner that they may be easily reached, in the order in which they are required for service. Each store-ship should be marked, at the bow and stern, on both sides, in large characters, with a distinctive letter and number. A list is to be made of the stores on board of each vessel, and of the place where they are to be found in it; a copy of this list to be sent to the chief officer of the proper department in the expedition, or at the place of destination.

BATTLES.

Before the action, the quartermaster of the division makes all the necessary arrangements for the transportation of the wounded. He establishes the ambulance depots in the rear, and gives his assistants the necessary instruction for the service of the ambulance wagons and other means of removing the wounded.

The ambulance depot, to which the wounded are carried or directed for immediate treatment, is generally established at the most convenient building nearest the field of battle. A *red flag* marks its place, or the way to it, to the conductors of the ambulances and to the wounded who can walk.

The active ambulances follow the troops engaged to succor the wounded and remove them to the depots; for this purpose the conductors should always have the necessary assistants, that the soldiers may have no excuse to leave the ranks for that object.

The medical director of the division, after consultation with the Quartermaster-General, distributes the medical officers and hospital attendants at his disposal, to the depots and active ambulances. He will send officers and attendants, when practicable, to the active ambulances, to relieve the wounded who require treatment before being removed from the ground. He will see that the depots and ambulances are provided with the necessary apparatus, medicines, and stores. He will take post and render his professional services at the principal depot.

If the enemy endanger the depot, the quartermaster takes the orders of the General to remove it or to strengthen its guard.

The wounded in the depots and the sick are removed, as soon as possible, to the hospitals that have been established by the

Quartermaster-General of the army on the flanks or rear of the army.

After an action, the officers of ordnance collect the munitions of war left on the field, and make a return of them to the General. The Quartermaster's Department collects the rest of the public property captured, and makes the return to head-quarters.

BAGGAGE TRAINS.

The baggage train of general head-quarters and the trains of the several divisions are each under the charge of an officer of the Quartermaster's Department. These officers conduct and command the trains under the orders they receive from their respective head-quarters. When the trains of different divisions march together, or the train of a division marches with the train of general head-quarters, the senior quartermaster directs the whole.

The Assistant-Quartermaster has charge of the wagons, horses, equipments, and all means of transport employed in the service of the regiment. Under the orders of the Colonel, he assembles them for the march, and maintains the order and police of the train in park and on the march. On marches, the regimental trains are under the orders of the quartermaster of the division. When the march is by brigade, the senior Assistant-Quartermaster in the brigade, or the quartermaster of the brigade, has the direction of the whole. The necessary wagon-masters, or non-commissioned officers to act as such, are employed with the several trains.

None but the authorized wagons are allowed to march with the train. The wagons of the several head-quarters, the regimental wagons and the wagons of sutlers authorized by orders from head-quarters to march with the train, are all to be conspicuously marked.

When the train of head-quarters is to have a guard, the strength of the guard is regulated by the General. Generals of Brigade guard their trains by the men attached to the train of the first regiment of their brigades. The regimental trains are loaded, unloaded, and guarded, as far as practicable, by convalescents and men not effective in the ranks; in the cavalry, by dismounted men. When the guard of a train is the escort for its defence, the regulations in regard to convoys and escorts take effect.

Habitually each division is followed by its train, the regimental train uniting at the brigade rendezvous. When otherwise, the order for the movement of the divisions, brigades and regiments, contains the necessary directions in regard to the assembling and marching of the respective trains The several trains march in an order analogous to the rank of the generals, and the order of battle of the troops to which they belong. Trains are not allowed in any case to be in the midst of the troops, or to impede the march of the troops.

The wagon-masters, under the orders of the officers of the Quartermaster's Department, exercise the necessary restraints over the teamsters and servants who leave their teams, or do not properly conduct them; or who ill-treat their horses, or who attempt to pillage, or run away in case of an attack.

The officers of the Quartermaster's Department, the wagon-masters, and all conductors of trains, are charged with watching that the regulations respecting transportation allowances are strictly observed.

REGULATIONS.

ADJ'T AND INSP'R GENERAL'S OFFICE,
RICHMOND, VA., Aug. 1861.

1. The following Regulations are published for the guidance of the Army, and they will be strictly enforced:

DISCHARGES.

2. No enlisted man shall be discharged before the expiration of his term of enlistment, without authority of the War Department, except by sentence of a general court-martial, or by the commander of the department, or of an army in the field, on certificate of disability, or on application of the soldier after twenty years' service.

3. When an enlisted man is to be discharged, his company commander shall furnish him certificates of his account, according to Form 5, pay department.

4. Whenever a non-commissioned officer or soldier shall be unfit for the military service, in consequence of wounds, disease or infirmity, his captain shall forward to the commander of the department, or of the army in the field, through the commander of the regiment or post, a statement of his case, with a certificate of his disability signed by the senior surgeon of the hospital, regiment or post, according to the form prescribed in the medical regulations.

5. If the recommendation for the discharge of the invalid be approved, the authority therefor will be endorsed on the "certificate of disability," which will be sent back to be completed and signed by the commanding officer, who will then send the same to the Adjutant General's office.

6. The date, place, and cause of discharge of a soldier absent from his company, will be reported by the commander of the post to his company commander.

7. Company commanders are required to keep the blank discharges and certificates carefully in their custody.

8. In no case will leaves of absence be granted so that a company be left without one of its commissioned officers, or that a garrison post be left without two commissioned officers and competent medical attendance; nor shall leave of absence be granted to an officer during the season of active operations, except on urgent necessity, and then as follows: the commander of a post may grant seven days' leave, the commander of an army thirty days.

9. When not otherwise specified, leaves of absence will be considered as commencing on the day that the officer is relieved from duty at his post. He will report himself monthly, giving his address, for the next thirty days, to the commander of his post, and of his regiment or corps, and to the Adjutant General; and in his first report state the day when his leave of absence commenced; at the expiration of his leave he will join his station.

10. The immediate commander of the officer applying for leave of absence, and all intermediate commanders, will endorse their opinion on the application before forwarding it.

11. The commander of a post may take leave of absence not to exceed seven days at one time, or in the same month, reporting the same fact to his next superior.

12. An application for leave of absence on account of sickness must be accompanied by a certificate of the senior medical officer present, in the following form: ——— ——— of the ——— regiment of ———, having applied for a certificate, on which to ground an application for leave of absence, I do hereby certify that I have carefully examined this officer and find that ———. (Here the nature of the disease, wound, or disability is to be fully stated, and the period during which the officer has suffered under its effects.) And that, in consequence thereof, he is, in my opinion, unfit for duty. I further declare my belief that he will not be able to resume his duties in a less period than ———. (Here state candidly and explicitly the opinion as to the period which will probably elapse before the officer will be able to resume his duties. When there is no reason to expect a recovery, or when the prospect of recovery is distant and uncertain, or when a change of climate is recommended, it must be so stated.) Dated at ———, this ——— day of ———.

SIGNATURE OF THE MEDICAL OFFICER.

13. When an officer is prevented by sickness from joining his station, he will transmit certificates in the above form monthly, to the commanding officer of his post and his regiment or corps, and to the Adjutant General; and when he cannot procure the certificates of a medical officer of the army, he will substitute his own certificate on honor to his condition, and a full statement of his case. If the officer's certificate is not satisfactory, and whenever an officer has been absent on account of sickness for one year, he shall be examined by a medical board, and the case specially reported to the President.

14. In all reports of absence, or applications for leave of absence on account of sickness, the officer shall state how long he has been absent already on that account, and by whose permission.

FURLOUGHS TO ENLISTED MEN.

15. Furloughs will be granted only by the commanding officer of the post, or the commanding officer of the regiment actually quartered with it. Furloughs may be prohibited at the discretion of the officer in command.

16. Soldiers on furlough shall not take with them their arms or accoutrements.

FORM OF FURLOUGH.

To all whom it may concern:

17. The bearer hereof ——— ———, a sergeant (corporal or private, as the case may be,) of Captain ——— ——— company, —— regiment of ———; age —— years, —— feet —— inches high, ——— complexion, —— eyes, —— hair, and by profession a ———; born in the —— of ——, and enlisted at ———, in the —— of ——, on the —— day of —— eighteen hundred and ——, to serve for the period of ———, is hereby permitted to go to ——— in the county of ———, State of ———, he having received a furlough from the —— day of —— to the —— day of ——, at which period he will rejoin his company or regiment at ——, or wherever it may be, or be considered a deserter.

Subsistence has been furnished to said ——— to the —— day of ——, and pay to the —— day of ——, both inclusive.
Given under my hand at ——, this —— day of ——, 18 .
Signature of the officer giving the furlough ————.
By command of Secretary of War.

S. COOPER,
Adjutant and Inspector General.

CONFEDERATE STATES OF AMERICA,
QUARTERMASTER GENERAL'S DEPARTMENT,
Richmond, Va., September 19, 1861.

The following Regulations having been adopted by the Secretary of War, are hereby promulgated for the information of the Army.

DESERTERS.

If a soldier desert from, or a deserter be received at, any post other than the station of the company or detachment to which he belonged, he shall be promptly reported by the commanding officer of such post to the commander of his company or detachment. The time of desertion, apprehension, and delivery will be stated. If the man be a recruit, unattached, the required report will be made to the Adjutant General.

When a report is received of the apprehension or surrender of a deserter at any post, other than the station of the company or detachment to which he belonged, the commander of such company or detachment shall immediately forward his description and account of clothing to the officer making the report.

A reward of thirty dollars will be paid for the apprehension and delivery of a deserter to an officer of the Army at the most convenient post or recruiting station. Rewards thus paid will be promptly reported by the disbursing officer to the officer commanding the company in which the deserter is mustered, and to the authority competent to order his trial.

The reward of thirty dollars will include the remuneration for all expenses incurred for apprehending, securing and delivering a deserter.

When non-commissioned officers or soldiers are sent in pursuit of a deserter, the expenses necessarily incurred will be paid, whether he be apprehended or not, and reported as in case of rewards paid.

Deserters shall make good the time lost by desertion, unless discharged by competent authority.

No deserter shall be restored to duty without trial, except by the authority competent to order the trial.

Rewards and expenses paid for apprehending a deserter, will be set against his pay, when adjudged by a court martial, or when he is restored to duty without trial on such condition.

In reckoning the time of service, and the pay and allowances of a deserter, he is to be considered in service when delivered up as a deserter to the proper authority.

An apprehended deserter, or one who surrenders himself, shall receive no pay while waiting trial, and only such clothing as may be actually necessary for him.

A. C. MYERS,
Quartermaster General.

CONFEDERATE STATES OF AMERICA,
QUARTERMASTER GENERAL'S DEPARTMENT,
Richmond, September 30, 1861.

The following decision of the Secretary of War is published for the information of all concerned:

Volunteers who have received the $21 commutation money for clothing under the act of Congress passed March 21, 1861, will be paid on the Muster Rolls of October 31st, 1861, the additional $4 allowed by the act recently passed, August 30, 1861. The sum of $25 will thereafter be paid on the same account for every additional six months' service.

A. C. MYERS,
Quartermaster General.

www.ingramcontent.com/pod-product-compliance
Lightning Source LLC
Chambersburg PA
CBHW030400170426
43202CB00010B/1441
* 9 7 8 3 3 3 7 7 1 3 6 5 2 *